THE GUNS OF MUSCHU

THE GUNS OF MUSCHU

DON DENNIS

ALLEN & UNWIN

To all those who have served in Australia's Special Forces

First published in Australia and New Zealand in 2006

Allen & Unwin
83 Alexander Street
Crows Nest NSW 2065
Australia
Phone: (61 2) 8425 0100
Fax: (61 2) 9906 2218
Email: info@allenandunwin.com

National Library of Australia
Cataloguing-in-Publication entry:

Dennis, D. J. (Donald James), 1945- .
The guns of Muschu.
ISBN 978 1 74114 878 7.

ISBN 1 74114 878 2.

1. Dennis, Mick. 2. World War, 1939-1945 - Papua New Guinea - Muschu - Personal narratives, Australian. 3. World War, 1939-1945 - Papua New Guinea - Muschu - Participation, Australian. 4. World War, 1939-1945 - Campaigns - Papua New Guinea - Muschu. I. Title.

940.548194

Maps by Don Dennis
Set in 12/18 pt AIProspera Book by Bookhouse, Australia

10 9 8 7 6 5 4 3 2 1

CONTENTS

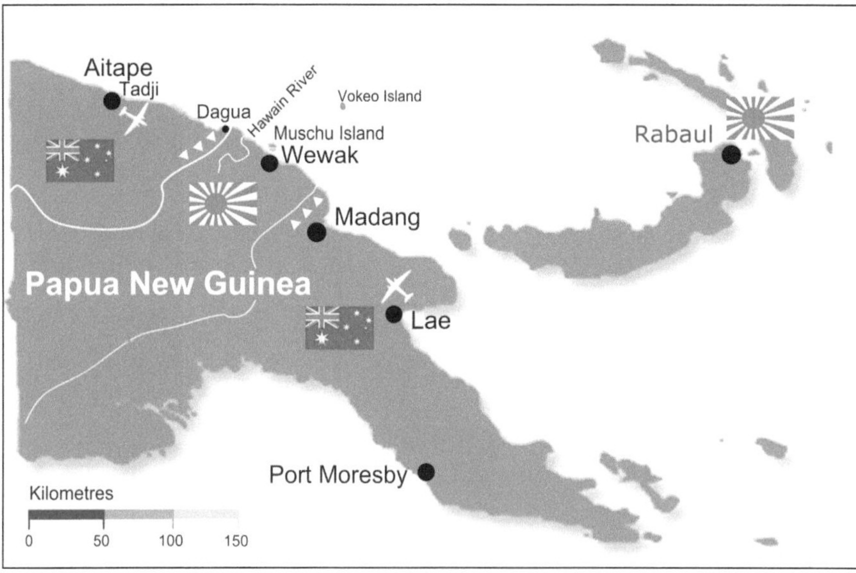

Aitape
Tadji
Dagua
Hawain River
Vokeo Island
Muschu Island
Wewak
Rabaul
Madang
Papua New Guinea
Lae
Port Moresby
Kilometres
0
50
100
150

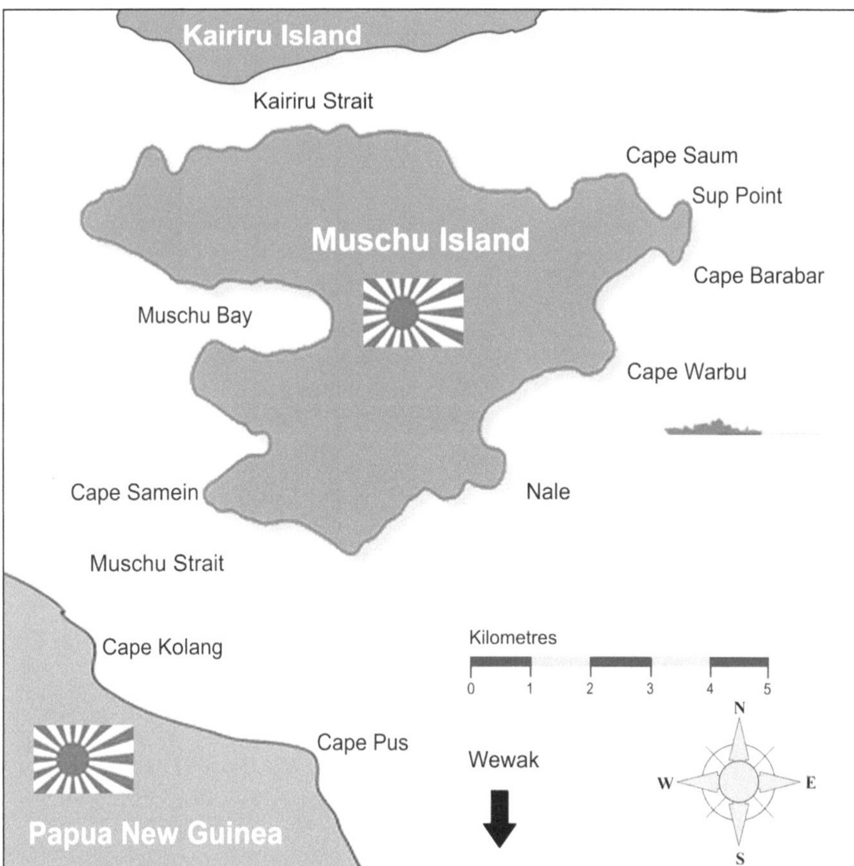

Kairiru Island
Kairiru Strait
Cape Saum
Sup Point
Muschu Island
Cape Barabar
Muschu Bay
Cape Warbu
Cape Samein
Nale
Muschu Strait
Cape Kolang
Kilometres
0
1
2
3
4
5
N
Cape Pus
Wewak
W
E
S
Papua New Guinea

1. TADJI, PNG:

2 MARCH 1945

From the cockpit of the Australian Beaufort A9-572, Flight Sergeant Ron Smith stared at the aircraft's starboard wing. A fist-sized hole had suddenly blossomed inboard of the engine and through the jagged metal he could see the jungle streaming past only a hundred feet below.

Smith's first reaction was outrage that the Japanese gunners should damage his aircraft, but this quickly turned to fear as another shell punched through the engine cowl and tore out the fuel lines. Both rounds exploded above the cockpit, ripping shrapnel through the perspex and shattering the instrument panel—one fragment slicing the glove across the back of his left hand before lodging in the prismatic compass.

Smith had no time to dwell on his luck: he now had his hands full controlling the aircraft. Even though the starboard engine stopped when the second round ripped through the fuel lines, the propeller continued turning in the slipstream. He tried the propeller's feather control but it refused to work. Quickly he opened the throttle on the remaining engine, but the combined effect of dead-engine drag and added power swung the aircraft wildly to the right. To compensate he shoved in the left rudder and aileron, creating more drag that needed even more power. He nudged the boost lever forward until the big Pratt & Whitney radial was delivering its maximum, but even then the aircraft barely maintained altitude.

Smith was no stranger to the Beaufort: in the six months he'd been with the squadron he'd chalked up almost 400 hours on the aircraft. Before that he'd flown Beaufighters for a year—also in New Guinea. It was a faster and more powerful development of the Beaufort, so in anyone's language he was rated as an experienced combat pilot. But now he was faced with a situation that would require all his experience if he and his crew were to survive.

This morning's mission had begun as most had, with a briefing in the 7th Squadron operations room at Tadji, in the Upper Sepik region of Papua New Guinea, before first light. Here, surrounded by aerial photos, maps and weather charts, the Operations Officer outlined reports from coastwatchers, intelligence agents and Army units advancing on the Japanese-held port of Wewak 150 kilometres down the coast. Today's mission was the 'usual' squadron raid—nine Beauforts would take off at dawn, gather into formation over the sea, then head for Wewak at 4000 feet. Ten minutes from the target, all aircraft would descend to 500 feet, then cross inland to pick up the run-in marker north of the port and from there, in groups of three, they'd make their attacks.

Australian coastwatchers had reported a Japanese freighter stealing into harbour the previous night, and the raid had been timed so that all aircraft arrived over the port just after sunrise. With luck they'd catch the freighter still unloading, hopefully with plenty of enemy soldiers and vehicles in the open as they tried to disperse the cargo. This was part of the strategy of denying the Japanese essential supplies, and destroying those that did make it through the naval blockade. For this raid all aircraft carried a load of two 250-kilogram and four 120-kilogram bombs—the smaller bombs fused to surface-detonate and cause maximum casualties among the dock workers.

Smith was leading a V formation of three aircraft that had been assigned the dock area. For he and his crew, this mission was just another in what now seemed to be an endless series of raids. However, although they'd made the Wewak run many times, they treated every mission as though it was their first. They knew that complacency was as much a danger as the enemy, and that one momentary slip could turn luck against them.

Wewak was a hive of anti-aircraft fire, and although they'd have an element of surprise, their approach would be reported and every Japanese soldier for miles around would be alerted to their arrival. Over the target they could expect to be met with everything from small arms to 80 mm anti-aircraft fire, much of which was deadly accurate. To minimise their exposure, all aircraft would hug the ground, drop their bombs at low level, then escape out to sea where they'd assess the attack and if necessary select targets of opportunity and hit them again.

That morning the briefing, aircraft pre-flights and take-off went as planned, with no delays or last-minute mechanical problems that often left one or more aircraft behind. The squadron climbed out into the rising sun—an irony not lost on Smith—then turned south over the sea and set course for Wewak, 20 minutes away. To the west, the Torricelli Mountains were cloaked in mist that clung to the trees like a white veil; ahead, the sky was clear, with only a few cloud smudges on the horizon to indicate the storms that would build later in the day.

There was the usual after take-off chatter over the intercom as the crew settled into the mission—the navigator in his nose compartment cross-checking with the pilot to ensure their instruments were in sync, the wireless operator in the compartment behind the pilot tuning his equipment and the gunner in the dorsal turret tapping off a few test rounds from his twin .303 calibre machine guns. All were part of a ritual that not only served to confirm that everything was functioning correctly, but also helped calm the crew's nerves.

Ten minutes into the flight, an eerie silence descended among the crew. It was always this way when they approached the halfway mark. From here on the situation became deadly serious. Smith shifted in his seat and loosened his seat harness slightly. He had a habit of doing this. Even though the full-body Sutton harness was vital for protection, the straps also restricted movement to such an extent that it could actually hamper a pilot's reach. Experience had taught him to compromise.

Today the three aircraft he was leading comprised the second group in the formation. He watched the lead group a hundred metres ahead, the three aircraft holding tight station on each other in the calm air over the sea. He remembered such a moment only a month back when they'd drawn fire from Japanese guns and one Beaufort suddenly erupted in a flash of greasy yellow fire. His own plane had flown through the heart of the explosion, only some singed paint and a slight shudder marking the spot where four men died.

Experiences like that worried Smith the most. If a Japanese shell found the bombload, it didn't matter how experienced or clever a pilot was—it would be 'game over' in the blink of an eye. At least if a plane sustained damage in an attack, the pilot had a fighting chance of controlling the aircraft and making it back to base in one piece.

But suddenly that morning, Smith doubted his own theory.

The attack had gone as planned. Five minutes from Wewak the formation descended to 500 feet and flew inland. There they used a prominent hill as a navigation marker, turned south and spread out into their attack groups. Smith's navigator then called the course to the target and he'd banked the aircraft onto the heading, then opened the throttles until the airspeed reached 300 kilometres an hour. With the two other aircraft in his section streaming astern at 500-metre intervals, he pressed lower until they were skimming the treetops.

Beneath the Beaufort the ground unravelled like a green conveyor belt, the hills giving way to neat squares of palm plantations near the coast. Sighting a road, Smith checked his course, then saw the harbour ahead and lined up on a row of warehouses. There was no sign of the freighter mentioned in the briefing—it had probably left the harbour before dawn. The dock area was stacked with cargo, a line of trucks suddenly breaking ranks as warning of the approaching aircraft sounded.

Smith held the Beaufort steady and aimed at the cargo stacks. Howling low over the dock, he heard the navigator call 'bombs gone' and felt the aircraft lurch as the load fell clear. Behind him the dorsal gunner's twin 303s were hammering away and in the nose the navigator joined in with his .50 calibre, the stench of cordite filling the cockpit. Banking further right to track along another line of warehouses, he sensed rather than heard the impact of the bombs behind them. Flicking off the gun safety, he pressed the yoke fire button and opened up with the two wing-mounted .50-calibre machine guns. Using the tracer to aim, he emptied the rounds into the waterfront buildings before banking left over the port and swinging into a wide turn that took them out to sea.

It was then that they were hit.

■ ■ ■

Later analysis revealed that the Japanese had been observing the behaviour of the Australian aircraft for some time and had noticed their tendency to use prominent turning points during their attacks. This was a standard procedure, essential to maintain orientation during group operations—not only did it allow pilots to quickly identify their position, but it also helped prevent aircraft from getting in each other's way in an unordered melee around the target. The Australians were well aware of the risks involved with becoming predictable and varied their attack patterns whenever possible.

However, that day it was the Japanese who struck it lucky. With a cluster of anti-aircraft weapons concentrated on a known turning point, Smith's aircraft was hit by two shells, possibly of 80 mm calibre. Fortunately the fuses of the Japanese shells were faulty, probably due to prolonged storage in damp tropical conditions, so instead of exploding on impact—which would have blown the Beaufort's wing off—the shells ripped through the aircraft before detonating.

For Smith, however, this was of little comfort. He now had a battle just to keep his plane in the air. At the best of times the Beaufort was notoriously sluggish on one engine, but when combined with battle damage it became a losing struggle against gravity, and the aircraft was now almost uncontrollable. With maximum boost on the port engine, the thrust was swinging the plane to the right. To compensate, Smith had his foot jammed on the left rudder pedal and the yoke held hard over in a vain attempt to drag the aircraft straight. He'd managed to complete the turn and they were now at 200 feet over the water about 4 kilometres off the coast, heading north. Ahead on the left he could see the port, part of the dock area now burning with thick oily smoke drifting inland, driven by a gentle sea breeze.

The other aircraft in his section were nowhere to be seen.

He thumbed the intercom button and tried talking to the crew, but the circuit was dead. Forward he could see his navigator in his seat, looking anxiously back at him. The navigator pressed his throat microphones to his neck, spoke briefly, then raised two fingers and gave a thumbs-up, indicating that the radio operator and dorsal gunner were OK.

Smith nodded back, then pointed ahead with his right hand. The course they were on would take them between the port and the island of Muschu, but with the unbalanced thrust from the remaining engine they were swinging further out to sea. Suddenly, the entire airframe shuddered, swinging the plane even further to the right. A glance at the damaged engine told him why—the engine mount had fractured and the entire assembly was now drooping, adding even more drag.

Now they were in real trouble. The aircraft seemed to be drawn towards the eastern end of Muschu Island like iron to a magnet and there was a risk that they would slam into the hills. He couldn't climb, he couldn't turn and they were too low to bail out. All he could do was throttle back and hope it would allow the aircraft to swing away from its collision course. In doing so he would lose precious altitude, but he had no choice.

Smith snatched the throttle, eased off power and felt the aircraft slowly swing away. The island was closing in fast. Hilly and green, with white beaches surrounded by clear blue lagoons, it looked more like a scene from a tourist brochure than an enemy haven. They would pass so low they'd be looking up at the small hills that bounded its eastern end. It was going to be close.

Palm trees blurred past the starboard wing. Glimpses of vines, shadows and light. A cleared area under the trees on the side of the hill. Japanese soldiers pointing. Machine guns surrounded by sandbags. A fleeting glimpse of two large guns beneath camouflage nets.

Tracer fire winked up at them. Bullets slammed into the aircraft, ripping more holes into the wing. Then finally they were past, a few tracers snapped by and floated off into the distance.

They were down to 100 feet and Smith could see the aircraft's shadow skimming the water's surface. He shoved the throttle wide open and the engine responded. The descent slowed, then stopped 50 feet above the water. For a moment he allowed himself to breathe easier, but he knew their problems were far from over. The aircraft was still trying to head out to sea and it was taking all his strength to keep the left rudder pedal shoved to the firewall. He doubted he could keep this up for the 30 minutes or more it would take to get back to Tadji airfield.

A quick check of the instruments told him that they were on borrowed time. The hydraulic pressure was zero, which meant the wheels couldn't be lowered, which in turn meant a belly-landing. That was not a good idea: Tadji's steel-plank runway had a habit of ripping aircraft apart, as well as creating sparks that ignited leaking fuel. Even if they did walk away from the wreck, there'd be hell to pay—the damage would put the strip out of action for hours and the Commanding Officer would not be pleased. Squadron standing orders were to crash anywhere except on the runway.

One option was dropping the aircraft into the jungle canopy, a technique used by some Army light observation aircraft—but hardly a choice in an aircraft the size of a Beaufort. Another was ditching in the ocean. Of the two, ditching was preferable, but was not without its dangers, for although the procedure was described in the flight manual in simple terms Smith knew it was far from so. And then there was the small matter of the sharks—the water along the coast was infested with them, mostly big, ugly hammerheads. However, even being chased by man-eaters seemed preferable to crashing and burning.

But Smith had little time to consider the options. Already the temperature gauges were hard against their stops, while the engine was trailing a thickening haze of blue smoke and emitting strange metallic noises. He signalled his navigator to tell the crew to make ready to ditch.

Everyone on board had trained for the procedure. It was a simple matter of the radio operator and dorsal gunner taking positions against the fuselage bulkhead facing the tail. The navigator's position was in a jump seat at the right of the pilot where he could assist with the controls, since Smith needed both hands on the yoke if he was to keep the aircraft straight when it hit the water.

Fortunately they were already heading into wind—a 10-knot nor'-easter by the look of the sea. Lining up, Smith aimed for a position between the shallow wave troughs about a kilometre off the mainland. He pumped at the flap lever. Slowly they lowered, but at fifteen degrees they stopped. Shoving hard on the lever, the flaps moved a few more degrees then jammed.

With only part flap they'd be landing hot. They'd hit the water at 100 kilometres an hour. Fast but not impossible.

No point using the altimeter, he noted, glancing at the shattered instrument. He guessed they were down to about 30 feet and he'd have to do everything by feel: even the airspeed indicator was useless.

The water rushed past, clear and smooth, making it difficult to judge height. He could clearly see the sandy bottom and to his left the aircraft's shadow, racing up to meet them. At what he estimated to be 15 feet above the water he hauled back the yoke.

The nose came up, but still the Beaufort kept flying, hanging on the Pratt & Whitney, which was now screaming in its final moments of over-boosted torment. Smith felt the shudder of an approaching stall and called to the navigator to close the throttle. The navigator dragged back the lever, then flicked the electric's master switch. The engine died and for a moment the sudden quiet seemed overwhelming, replaced by the gentle whisper of the slipstream.

Smith had timed the landing perfectly. Nose high, the Beaufort stalled, then hit the water tail-first. He braced, crossed his arms in front of his face and held on to the canopy frame. The next few seconds were a montage of whirling sky, water and sound. He later likened it to being inside a washing machine.

The aircraft pitched forward, nosed under then recoiled, throwing Smith hard against his harness. Then there was silence punctuated by the hiss of water on hot metal.

Behind him, the navigator slammed open the escape hatch. Smith turned to see his feet vanishing through the opening and heard him splash overboard. Glancing down he saw the cockpit floor was already covered in water. They were sinking. With strength inspired by fear, Smith dragged himself from his seat, but a harness strap caught around his thigh. The water was now over his feet and he could hear it gurgling in. Reaching down to his left boot, he gripped the stubby shroud knife he kept sheathed there, dragged it out and sliced through the harness. The strap parted and he struggled free.

Wedging through the narrow gap at the top of the seat, he scrambled up through the shattered canopy and slid head-first into the water between the nose and the port engine. He went under, then felt the aircraft bump past him as it sank. The tailplane slammed into his back then snagged his trouser leg, dragging him with it. Through the clear water he could see the aircraft below him, streaming bubbles as it headed for the bottom with him attached. With the strength of desperation, he put both feet on the tailplane and shoved. He tore free and with lungs bursting, clawed for the surface.

He popped up to find his crew sitting in two life rafts, paddles in hand, looking at him with concerned expressions.

Ten minutes later the crew of Beaufort A9-572 were aboard an American torpedo boat heading back to Aitape, the main Australian base on the north-east coast of New Guinea.

2. SIXTH DIVISION HQ, AITAPE, PNG:
2 MARCH 1945

Captain Roland McKay was the officer in command of the division's intelligence section. As the G3 Intelligence, McKay directed a staff of fifteen who were responsible for assessing information gathered by units within the division and other agencies in Australia. Located in a row of iron-roofed huts scattered in a grove of palm trees near the headquarters area, the intelligence section was an around-the-clock operation, continually monitoring the enemy's capabilities and trying to anticipate their intentions. To do this McKay enjoyed a level of autonomy not generally shared by other officers, and this independence enabled him to travel wherever he wanted within the operational area and to gain access to senior officers or the lowliest private soldier almost without question.

Responsible to the G2—the senior operations officer on the headquarters staff—McKay had established a reputation as a quiet, intense analyst with a bloodhound-like ability to pursue the tiniest scrap of information. A lawyer before the war, he was aged 29 when he joined the Australian Imperial Force in 1940. Categorised as unfit for active service due to the effects of poliomyelitis as a child that left him with a slight limp, he'd been recruited by the Intelligence Corps, commissioned as a lieutenant and spent the next three years in a department of the Allied South West Pacific headquarters in Australia, where he'd gained an intimate knowledge of the organisational structure of all allied intelligence agencies. Policy in this regard was strict: anyone with such knowledge was considered a security risk if allowed into an operational area, and they were subsequently restricted to mainland postings. Such personnel were often unfairly labelled 'koalas'—not to be exported or shot at—and although McKay understood the reasons behind such restrictions, it didn't stop him from trying to gain a transfer to an operational unit. Every month he'd routinely submit an application and every month it would be refused.

However, McKay persisted and in June 1944, with the war turned in Australia's favour, his badgering paid off. The restrictions were relaxed and he was sent to Aitape as part of the headquarters group, to prepare for the final push against the Japanese in New Guinea.

■ ■ ■

It was 1500 hours when McKay received a phone call from the Army Liaison Officer (ALO) attached to the Australian Air Force's Tactical Operations Centre at Tadji airfield. The ALO was a lieutenant with whom he'd formed a close working relationship and who normally at this time gave him a rundown on the day's air activity for the division commander's 1600 hours briefing. Today, however, the ALO advised that he'd received information that might affect preparations for a coming operation and a copy was already being couriered to Divisional Intelligence.

Curiosity roused, McKay thanked him then rang off. He glanced through the blast-taped window of the corrugated iron hut. The sun was breaking through rain clouds to the west, painting the Torricelli Mountains with intense colour. A shower had just passed over, cooling the air and settling the dust. The roads would now be slick with mud and vehicles were already sliding on the greasy surfaces. In an hour the mud would again be dust and the air would be heavy with humidity.

Leaning back in his chair, McKay wondered what the ALO considered so important that he was reluctant to explain it over the landline. The nearest Japanese were more than 40 kilometres away and were hardly in a position to eavesdrop. Yet he also knew such caution was never wasted—hundreds of kilometres of cable were strung around the base, out to Tadji airfield and to the battalions operating inland. The Japanese were clever with things electronic, so anything was possible.

Only one operation planned warranted such concern. Since January, Divisional Intelligence had been gathering information for an amphibious landing to capture the port town of Wewak, on the east coast of Papua New Guinea. Scheduled for May, this would pit some 6000 Australians against the remainder of the Japanese 21st and 51st divisions—an estimated 15,000 in the Wewak area. Although conventional military wisdom was to ensure the attacking force had a three-to-one advantage, the operation was expected to be completed quickly and with minimal casualties.

Part of this confidence came from the knowledge that the Sixth Division's plan called for a multi-pronged assault that concentrated forces where they'd have a numerical advantage. Coupled with an element of surprise, plus overwhelming air superiority, they'd divide the enemy's forces and prevent them mounting a coherent defence. It was basically a simple plan—a virtue in itself, as complex battle plans tended to unravel on contact with the enemy.

However, assessments of the Japanese capability to fight varied. Weakened from battle and tropical disease, they were isolated, their supply line from Rabaul in the Papuan province of East New Britain disrupted by the Navy and Air Force. They were desperately short of food and many units were trying to survive by living off the land. In all areas, constant pressure by advancing Australian patrols backed by air support had driven the Japanese into isolated pockets and whittled their numbers. Some units were fighting as tenaciously as ever; others were surrendering after only token resistance.

There had been growing dissent among Australian troops about the need to continue the fight against the Japanese in some areas, fueled by rumours and press reports about arguments between the Chief of the Army, General Thomas Blamey, and Prime Minister John Curtin. These stories told how Curtin wanted to drop all plans for offensives against Wewak and Borneo. Curtin argued that the American invasion of Japan would take place before the end of the year, and as the Japanese would inevitably surrender, there was no point sacrificing Australian lives in operations that couldn't affect this outcome. He suggested the Japanese be bypassed and isolated until they either surrendered or died of starvation or disease.

For men fighting a vicious enemy in one of the ugliest campaigns of the war, to be suddenly offered an honourable end to the uncertainty of survival and maybe a quick return home, this was an attractive argument—after all, no one wanted to be the last to die in a campaign that was now considered unnecessary.

To confuse the issue, the debate had become clouded by soldierly conjecture and rumouring that Blamey was determined to cover his failings in the early days of the New Guinea campaign; he didn't want the Japanese escaping to breed with the natives to create a future problem; he wanted leverage at the peace table after the war so Australia could dominate the south-west Pacific. Curtin, meanwhile, was an alcoholic fool unable to stand up to Blamey, was under the control of left-wing unionists and was even dying of syphilis, according to one story.

Soldiers almost universally despise politicians, and Blamey was already unpopular with many New Guinea veterans. For the troops, this was a unique opportunity for double-barrelled criticism and they embellished these rumours in a way only Australians knew how, questioning why they were fighting a beaten enemy instead of leaving them to 'wither on the vine', as the press was so fond of quoting.

In response, Blamey's orders to the Sixth Division were uncompromising: ignore the rumours and proceed with preparations to take Wewak. All units were reminded that the Japanese were far from beaten and any slackening of pressure could see them go on the offensive in a wave of suicidal assaults that could cause more casualties than any proposed invasion.

However, one result of the mounting conjecture was that plans for the Wewak landings were continually being revised to minimise risk. For the intelligence staff, this meant thoroughly investigating any new information that might have a bearing on the enemy's ability to fight. Not necessarily a bad thing, McKay agreed, but one could only take it so far. It was, after all, a war—and in war men died no matter how thorough the planning.

A knock on the door interrupted his thoughts. A corporal clerk slipped a large brown envelope on the desk, then left. Opening it, McKay took out a single typed page and saw it was a copy of an aircrew debriefing concerning the loss of two Australian Beaufort bombers near Wewak that morning. It told how one of the aircraft, Beaufort A9-572, was damaged by anti-aircraft fire, then flew close to Muschu Island where it again came under fire. The crew of the damaged bomber described the enemy fire as consisting of heavy machine guns and possibly larger-calibre weapons. The pilot also claimed he saw two large artillery pieces near the crest of a hill at the eastern end of the island before ditching the aircraft. A note attached to the report, written by the ALO, explained that a tactical reconnaissance aircraft later sent out to confirm the sighting had found nothing.

McKay paused. The presence of artillery on Muschu Island had been an enigma for the past two years, and this could be the first confirmed sighting of the weapons. He glanced up at his wall map. Muschu was the closer of two islands off the coast of Wewak. Separated by a narrow strait from the larger island of Kairiru, both islands were known to have artillery on their high ground overlooking the sea approaches to both islands. The guns of Muschu, however, were in range of Wewak and could theoretically be used to support the defenders there.

About 4 kilometres from the mainland at its nearest point, Muschu was a flat island skirted by lagoons and beaches, 12 kilometres east to west and 7 kilometres north to south, with low hills at the eastern end. Used by the Japanese mainly as a food supply area, an estimated 700 Japanese were stationed there. These were mainly second-line troops occupied in growing crops, hunting game and catching fish to help supplement the Wewak garrison's food supply.

The guns on Muschu were believed to be located somewhere in the hills at the eastern end of the island. Installed shortly after Wewak's capture by the Japanese in 1942, it was assumed they were intended to cover the sea approaches to the port. Captured documents from a detachment of the Tokubetsu Konkyochitai—the naval command echelon—revealed that they were 140 mm naval guns manufactured in 1916. Although old, they were still excellent weapons: copies of a British Vickers design, they were rated more effective than the original, with a maximum range of almost 20,000 metres. However, reports from the US Navy, which had exchanged fire with them in 1943, indicated that the guns were hopelessly inaccurate. Since then they hadn't fired a shot.

The reasons for this only became apparent in late 1944. A diary taken from a captured Japanese artillery officer noted that he'd spent six months on Muschu as part of the gunnery team. He described the gun battery as beset with problems, including second-rate gun crews, and lack of fire-control equipment such as rangefinders and gunnery calculators. Reports from other sources supported the diary, including information captured from a Japanese engineer unit describing how the gun mounts were on unstable ground and couldn't withstand the shock of firing. Attempts to reinforce the mounts had failed—there wasn't enough concrete or reinforcing steel available. From this it was deduced that the battery would be ineffective in any coming actions and could be discounted as a significant threat.

Even so, there had been many attempts to locate the guns and put them out of action. The island had been kept under almost constant air reconnaissance, the Australian Navy regularly shelled the area, and the Air Force had flown bombing sorties over the island, peppering every likely gun position. It had been assumed that the guns, if they were still there, were either damaged or abandoned. But now that there had been an actual sighting, the pilot's description raised concerns in McKay's mind. If the guns were protected by anti-aircraft weapons, the Japanese clearly regarded them with some value. Could it be that the guns were still serviceable and the assessment of their capability was wrong?

McKay knew that at short range—about a kilometre—using open sights and aimed like a rifle, the guns could be deadly; any greater distance would require a large element of luck to hit a moving or even stationary target without rangefinders. These facts had already been taken into consideration. During the landings there'd be aircraft on call that could deal with the guns if they were foolish enough to fire on the invasion force. They'd be reduced to scrap within minutes of the first round leaving the barrel.

However, what now concerned him was that if the guns were defended, they might be harder to neutralise than anticipated, resulting in a longer duration of firing. One-third of the Australians, designated Florida Force, would be landing on a beach east of Wewak, well inside the range of the guns. With landing craft crowded into the area, even the most incompetent gun crew would eventually hit something—and a single strike by a 140 mm shell on a crowded deck could cause hundreds of casualties. Although they'd compromise their location and be blasted into scrap, it would be just the type of suicidal gesture that appealed to the Japanese.

It wasn't only the guns that were of concern. Prisoner-of-war interrogation, captured documents and wireless intercepts indicated that there'd been an increase in activity on the island. Unfortunately, accurate information about Muschu was scarce, and assessments of the actual strengths of the Japanese units on the island hadn't been revised for some time. Opening a file, McKay examined the latest Sixth Division Intelligence Summary for the area. Taken from documents captured on the mainland in February, the summary outlined the enemy dispositions on Muschu and Kairiru:

> A document and maps, dated 22–25 September 1944, deals with the defences of Kairiru-Muschu Islands in great detail. The troops allotted for the defence of Kairiru aren't detailed but the weapons allotted total 4 mountain guns, 22 13 mm guns, 22 heavy machine guns, and 13 light machine guns.
>
> Approximately 700 troops are named as forming the garrison on Muschu Island, made up of the following units:
>
> 63 Anti-Aircraft Unit
> 5 Shipping Engineer Unit
> 1 Company 115 Regt (Inf) and 1 Machine Gun Company
> 31 Machine Cannon Company
> 33 Machine Cannon Company
>
> It is considered that these elaborate defence measures were made when it was possible an amphibious operation might be mounted by United States forces, with their typical use of overpowering air and naval support. The garrison may not have subsequently been maintained at the same high strength.

It was generally agreed that the garrisons had not been kept up to their original strength, but as there was no doubt that the Japanese were anticipating the Australian attack on Wewak, exactly what role would Muschu now play in its defence? Were they going to use it to launch counterattacks on the Australians? Hardly likely due to the logistics involved, but still a possibility considering that the Japanese were in a suicidal frame of mind. Even a few determined men with explosive-laden barges or fishing boats could create havoc.

McKay concluded that it would be wise to find out exactly what was happening on Muschu. The best way would be to put in a reconnaissance patrol—men who could actually observe and report. Despite the best aerial cameras and the new electronic eavesdropping devices now in use, human observers were still the most reliable sources of information in a situation such as this. That would be a task for the Services Reconnaissance Department—a small unit of commandos also known as Z Special. They could get in, do the job, then get out again without the enemy even knowing they'd been there.

McKay had been involved with Z Special during his time with the South West Pacific Headquarters in Australia, when in September 1943, his department had helped gather information in preparation for Operation Jaywick. Using a captured Japanese fishing boat, the team had sailed from Darwin through Japanese-controlled waters to Malaya. There a raiding party paddled three canoes into Singapore Harbour, where they sank seven ships with limpet mines and then escaped without a casualty. Although this triumph had been hailed as justification of the special forces concept, Z Special's true value had subsequently been found to be in the reconnaissance role. Z Special now had its South West Pacific headquarters with the Australian 1st Army in Lae, and an operational detachment at Aitape.

McKay took a file from a locked desk drawer and checked the Services Reconnaissance Department patrol schedule. Muschu had been listed several times since late 1944, but priorities kept changing and the patrols had been reassigned to other areas. It was still on the 'to do' list, but a definite time had not yet been allocated. He made a note to recommend to the G2 Operations that, in light of the guns sighting and other information indicating increased activity on the island, Muschu should be given priority for reconnaissance by a Z Special patrol.

3. ALLIED INTELLIGENCE BUREAU, BRISBANE:

4 MARCH 1945

Tucked away in the basement of an old stone mansion in the suburb of Ascot Park, the No 1 Radio Intercept Unit was part of the intelligence network established by General Douglas MacArthur after the fall of the Philippines. Its existence known only to a few within the Allied Intelligence Bureau (AIB), the Radio Intercept Unit's cryptographers deciphered Japanese transmissions recorded by listening stations scattered around the Pacific.

Like its British 'Enigma' counterpart at Bletchley Park in the UK, which deciphered German radio traffic, the Pacific radio intercept network had become a vital source of information for the Australian and American intelligence services. Although only small by comparison to the British operation, its capabilities were extensive, mostly due to the technology developed by the British early in the war. Once the Americans entered the war and learned the secret behind Britain's electro-mechanical deciphering machines, they set about developing faster and more powerful equivalents. From an inconspicuous beginning in 1942, marred by rivalries between the

Americans, Australians and British, by 1945 the AIB was capable of deciphering most high-level Japanese coded traffic within a matter of hours.

Apart from high-level ciphered traffic, radio messages were also being transmitted in lesser codes, down to operators at unit level who spoke in the clear. These conversations would usually be conducted using military jargon, containing information of little immediate value to an eavesdropping opponent. However, where possible, these conversations were also monitored by Allied listening stations around the Pacific, where they were recorded, then passed on for translation and analysis.

It is commonly perceived that only information originating from the highest sources—such as the enemy headquarters—is of value. However, even low-level messages contain clues that when viewed together by a skilled analyst build a picture that reveals the enemy's intentions. Even information from the smallest unit is potentially valuable, so a great deal of effort went into monitoring what was known as the enemy's 'housekeeping' radio traffic. Every military force relies on its logistic chain to keep it functioning—everything from ammunition to paper clips must be supplied where and when it's needed. Deciphered, translated then classified, this administrative radio traffic, although mundane, continually added to the understanding of the enemy's situation. Unfortunately for the AIB, hundreds—or even thousands—of such messages were intercepted by the network each day. To stay abreast of this barrage of information using human resources alone was a huge logistical task.

To speed the deciphering process, the US Signal Corps developed punch-card machines capable of sorting information according to pre-set conditions. The forerunner of programmable computers, these IBM tabulating machines filled every available space in the basement of the Ascot building, then overflowed into the mansion's huge garage, with more machines installed in other buildings around the city. Even with the assistance of this new technology, the AIB's effectiveness ultimately depended on the human factor. While tabulating machines were capable of sorting the translated information, they weren't capable of recognising its meaning. That was left to specialists who would review the information, further categorise it, then direct it to Army, Navy or Air Force headquarters units, where local intelligence staff assessed how it fitted into their particular situation, then disseminated it further down the line. It was a continuous and often boring process, occasionally punctuated by a major event.

The Ascot Park building also housed eight area analysts, who scanned the categorised information to determine if it had any bearing on the areas they were assigned to monitor. This procedure, introduced early in 1943 to expedite the assessment process, had proven very successful. Six of these analysts were women, all respected by their male counterparts as exceptionally capable due to their uncanny memory and ability to discriminate between even the smallest of details.

■ ■ ■

On the morning of 4 March 1945, an hour after coming on duty, one of the women noticed an anomaly in the information she was reviewing. The night's tabulator run had resulted in a thick sheaf of printed messages being delivered to her cubicle—mostly translations of administrative radio traffic transmitted between Japanese units around Wewak, an area she had been monitoring for six months. Such was the precision of her memory that she knew the order of battle of all units, their approximate strengths, and even most of their commanders' names.

One series of messages contained a name she was familiar with, yet didn't quite fit the context she expected. The first message read: 'Order immediate recall of all 140 mm HE [High Explosive] ammunition from 14 Sempura battery. Have ready for transport by barge 2200 hours, 10th.' Signed, Watanabe, Colonel.

There followed a reply from the artillery unit objecting to their ammunition being commandeered. It was signed Yusho, Captain, 14 Sempura.

Colonel Watanabe's response came fifteen minutes later. 'Report immediately to my HQ, Muschu.'

For a moment the duty analyst allowed herself to dwell on Captain Yusho's predicament. The colonel sounded like a man not to be trifled with and Yusho would obviously face a severe dressing down for having questioned his order. However, her amusement was short lived as she realised something was out of place.

From a shelf she took down a directory of Japanese officers serving in New Guinea. This document was the result of an important intelligence breakthrough when, in late 1942, the capture of the Japanese Officer List by Australian Military Intelligence enabled the Allies to develop a detailed understanding of the command structure of the entire Japanese Army. Continually updated, it had been expanded to include the Japanese Navy and Air Force, with the career records and psychological profiles of most serving officers. Quickly flicking through to the name Watanabe, she saw that in the Wewak area there was one listing entered almost six months ago—but he was described as a lieutenant medical officer, not a colonel in command of an artillery unit.

During the past three months she had reviewed a number of messages originating from Watanabe, whom she deduced had been assigned to Muschu Island as the medical officer. From memory these were routine requests for supplies, health reports, manpower statistics—information a medical unit would be expected to provide its HQ on a regular basis.

But now Watanabe had revealed himself as a colonel. Even in the dwindling Japanese Army, promotion wasn't that quick. Also, he was ordering artillery ammunition to be withdrawn from a combat unit—edicts certainly beyond the scope of a medical officer.

This anomaly suggested that there had been a mix-up with Watanabe's original identification. Considering the amount of radio traffic the section dealt with, such errors were inevitable. The duty analyst made a note on a form advising of the possible error, put it in her out-tray, then returned her attention to the pile of printed messages.

■ ■ ■

It was almost midday when a file containing a list of updates from the duty analysts crossed the desk of the Second in Command of the Radio Intercept Unit, Lieutenant Commander David Mallory. Mallory made a point of reviewing the morning's work, then over the lunchbreak he'd discuss any points of interest with the staff. That morning he saw, among other items, the correction to the identity of Lieutenant Watanabe originated by the Wewak area analyst. Another analyst in the 'corrections group' had confirmed the error, noting that it was caused by a simple spelling mistake. There were in fact two Japanese officers: Lieutenant Wantanabe of the medical corps, and Lieutenant Colonel Watanabe, a staff officer on the headquarters of the 21st Division in Wewak. The confusion of identities was understandable, caused by similarities in spelling and rank.

The note went on to explain that Lieutenant Colonel Watanabe was already known to the AIB. An artillery officer, he was a veteran of the Manchurian campaign, had served in the Philippines and had last been heard of in General Iwao Matsuda's headquarters in January. The fact that he'd now shown up on the staff of the 21st Division in Wewak and had his own headquarters on Muschu Island posed some interesting questions.

Mallory was pleased to see that the error had come to light. Whether the information was important or not was best left up to the Sixth Division's intelligence staff to decide. He drafted a signal instructing all information be forwarded immediately to Sixth Division Intelligence at Aitape.

4. ALLIED TRANSLATOR AND INTERPRETER SERVICE, BRISBANE:

5 MARCH 1945

Located in the Brisbane suburb of Indooroopilly, the headquarters of the Allied Translator and Interpreter Service (ATIS) was housed in a large stone mansion with the tongue-twisting Scottish name of Tighnabruaich. A section within the Allied Intelligence Bureau, the ATIS had on staff more than 100 translators, most of them American-born Japanese sent to Australia for the duration. After training, many were posted to ATIS units attached to Australian and American forces throughout the Pacific, where they provided front-line translation services.

The Brisbane headquarters was also responsible for supplying translators to the Radio Intercept Unit and interrogating Japanese prisoners of war—mainly high-ranking personnel, or others suspected of possessing information of particular interest.

These prisoners would be flown to Brisbane from New Guinea or the Pacific Islands, then conveyed in secrecy to the mansion where the interrogation procedure began. For this purpose Tighnabruaich was perfect.

Built in 1892 and modelled after a Scottish laird's home and set in spacious grounds far from prying eyes, it was the type of building that chilled the imagination, with dozens of rooms, huge fireplaces, deep cellars and even hidden passages. Requisitioned by the military in 1942 and renamed Witton Barracks, it was guarded by a Military Police unit. Security was unobtrusive but tight, nearby civilian residents having no idea what transpired within the mansion's thick stone walls—or that over 300 Japanese had been interrogated there by the end of the war.

The morning of 5 March 1945, an interrogation team had just completed a 24-hour session with a recently arrived prisoner and had gathered to compile their final report. The transcript would then be typed and forwarded to analysts in the Allied Intelligence Bureau for examination, cross-referencing and distribution.

The prisoner in question was a Japanese naval lieutenant captured after his submarine was attacked by US Navy aircraft off the island of Luzon in the Philippines only a few days earlier. Twenty survivors had escaped the crippled submarine, the remainder of the crew electing to die with their ship. Rescued by a destroyer, the survivors included a young lieutenant who was found to be the boat's navigation officer. He was immediately separated from the rest of the crew, transferred to an aircraft carrier, then flown to the Philippines where he was blindfolded and loaded aboard a C-47 bound for Australia. Within 36 hours he was in the sterile surroundings of the Tighnabruaich 'confessional', being spoken to by friendly but firm Japanese men wearing American Army uniforms. The entire process was intended to disorient, confuse and intimidate. At this it was successful—the lieutenant conveyed almost his entire life's story to the smiling gentlemen in khaki after only a few hours of persuasion.

What had prompted his urgent interrogation was mounting US Navy intelligence indicating that the Japanese were intending to launch a mass attack of submarines against elements of the Pacific Fleet. It was estimated that the Japanese could gather about 20 submarines and stage a suicidal assault—more a gesture than anything else, but a costly one for the Americans if it proved successful. The Japanese lieutenant's vessel was suspected of being part of this assault.

However, the young lieutenant had a different story to tell. His submarine had been acting as a delivery service to the blockaded garrison at Wewak. Carrying twelve Long Lance torpedoes modified to hold cargo instead of explosives, they'd crept through the Allied naval patrols to within 10 nautical miles of the coast and launched all torpedoes on a track that beached them just south of the port. With each torpedo able to carry about 1000 kilograms, it was an expensive way of delivering supplies, but effective none the less.

When questioned as to what cargo the torpedoes were carrying, the lieutenant at first offered very little information. However, with gentle prompting, he did suddenly remember that his captain had at the last minute ordered him to supervise the placement of a small, well-wrapped parcel inside one of the torpedoes. What surprised the lieutenant was that the parcel contained two bottles of sake, addressed to a colonel whose name he clearly remembered as Watanabe. When coaxed, he was also able to give a rough description of what he saw in the torpedo's cargo space. He described the compartment as being full, most of it taken up by one large cylindrical package marked 'manufactured by Barr & Stroud'. The markings were in Japanese and English.

While this wasn't considered new information—the Japanese had used this supply delivery technique in other blockaded areas of the Pacific—the ATIS interrogators realised that some elements might be important. It didn't take long for ATIS staff to establish that Barr & Stroud was a Scottish engineering company that specialised in manufacturing precision military optical devices, including binoculars, telescopes and rangefinders. The Japanese Navy had purchased a large quantity of Barr & Stroud's rangefinders in 1902, which they'd put to very effective use in the Russian-Japanese war of 1904. From the lieutenant's description, the torpedo contained one of these early-model rangefinders, which although now obsolete, were still considered excellent instruments. A search through the department's library came up with a catalogue of Barr & Stroud products, and from the known dimensions of the Long Lance torpedo's warhead, as well as the Japanese lieutenant's description of the package, it was deduced that the rangefinder was a model JA1901, a double-prismatic binocular instrument capable of resolving ranges up to 18,000 metres.

The two bottles of sake consigned to Colonel Watanabe gave a clue as to who the rangefinder was intended for. A check of the New Guinea Japanese forces personnel listing revealed that Watanabe's record had been updated only a day earlier by the Allied Intelligence Bureau Radio Intercept Unit.

All this was duly noted, then forwarded to the Allied Intelligence Bureau HQ across the city in Queen Street. Within a few hours the report was being transmitted by encrypted radio to Sixth Division Intelligence in Aitape.

5. SIXTH DIVISION HQ, AITAPE:

6 MARCH 1945

Since the 2 March sighting of the guns on Muschu Island, daily sorties by reconnaissance aircraft had failed to confirm their location. Doubts were being expressed as to the validity of the original sighting: after a long search, one reconnaissance pilot reported seeing the charred trunks of two palm trees felled by naval gunfire that resembled gun barrels from certain angles.

Flight Sergeant Ron Smith, the pilot of the downed Beaufort, refused to accept that what he'd seen were palm trunks and, having recovered from a mild concussion, offered to fly as an observer in one of the reconnaissance aircraft. After cautiously recreating his last approach to the island several times, no guns were sighted. However, it was agreed that due to the heavy jungle canopy in the area, concealing two large guns from aerial reconnaissance would be relatively simple.

An Australian naval destroyer was called in to shell the high ground in an attempt to open up the canopy. After expending a hundred rounds of 105 mm ammunition with little effect on the foliage, the attempt was abandoned. Bombing the area by Beauforts using 120 kg bombs proved equally disappointing. By 5 March it was decided that perhaps the best course of action was to return to the original plan of dealing with the guns if they became active during the landings.

The G3 Intelligence, Captain Roland McKay, wasn't totally convinced. Since he'd first been prompted to look more closely at the island, he'd been receiving scattered pieces of information that indicated activity there had increased, including preparing defensive positions along the high ground at the eastern end overlooking possible landing areas. One suggestion was that a force should be landed on the island simultaneously with the main Wewak force; however, this would require at least a battalion, plus supporting elements. These could be better used in the main landings, rather than chasing a second-line enemy force around an isolated island.

While opinions still differed on the role Muschu would play in defending Wewak, it was agreed that there was a growing need to determine the actual situation there. Had the garrison been reduced or reinforced? What new defences had been constructed? Were there really naval guns on the island, or were they only a figment of someone's imagination? Maybe the entire situation was an elaborate diversion?

On the morning of 6 March, however, a series of messages arrived from Allied Intelligence Bureau departments in Australia which suddenly changed everything. After examining them McKay quickly noted, point by point, the information he now had.

Known facts:
The Muschu guns have been sighted on the hills at the eastern end of the island. Ongoing Tactical Reconnaissance has not been able to confirm this sighting due to heavy jungle.

Lieutenant Colonel Watanabe, an artillery specialist, has been on the HQ staff of the 21st Division since January (previously misidentified as a medical officer with a similar name).

Watanabe has a headquarters on Muschu Island.

Increased movement of personnel between Wewak and the island has been reported by natives and coastwatchers. It is uncertain whether there has been an increase or decrease in personnel on the island. Assessment is that the fittest personnel are being transferred to the Wewak garrison in exchange for some second-line personnel.

Administrative radio traffic has increased between the island and the HQ 21st Division. Our Signals Intelligence advise they are now operating on three radio channels within the High Frequency band. It is suspected the Japanese now have two, possibly more, transmission-receiving sites on the island, one of which is located at the western end, another halfway along the island. One is suspected to be a mobile (manpack) unit. Tactical Reconnaissance aircraft have not been able to locate any fixed antennas.

Stocks of telephone cable have recently been shipped to the island from Wewak. Indications are that more than 9 kilometres of cable have been delivered. This is consistent with the construction of new defensive positions and linking them to dispersed and central command centres.

A Jap engineering unit sent a construction team to the island in early February along with several bargeloads of supplies, some of which were reported by coastwatchers and trusted natives to be concrete and reinforcing steel.

Colonel Watanabe has ordered stocks of 140 mm ordnance moved from a shore battery to Muschu Island. (How many rounds?)

A British rangefinder (Barr & Stroud, model JA1901) was included in the cargo landed by torpedoes near Wewak. The B&S JA1901 is effective up to 18,000 metres.

Previous intelligence indicates the guns on Muschu are copies of a British Vickers design, 140 mm calibre with a maximum range of 15,000 to 20,000 metres.

Colonel Watanabe had two bottles of sake delivered in the same torpedo as the rangefinder. Was the rangefinder delivered in the storage torpedo destined for Watanabe? (Highly probable.)

McKay reflected that one of the basic rules of intelligence assessment is that often the obvious conclusion is the correct conclusion. For McKay, the obvious conclusion was that Colonel Watanabe had spent two months bringing the Muschu guns into service. He now had the rangefinders and calculating equipment required to lay them accurately and was acquiring ammunition stocks from mainland batteries. The guns were probably well defended from both ground and air attack and therefore could present a serious threat to the Wewak landing force.

McKay decided to strongly recommend the use of a Z Special patrol to confirm his findings. He gathered his notes and headed for the office of the G2 Operations—ultimately it would be his decision.

6. 1ST AUSTRALIAN ARMY HQ, LAE, PNG:
9 MARCH 1945

On 9 March a request from the General Officer Commanding (GOC) of the Sixth Division for a reconnaissance of Muschu Island was sent to the commander of the Services Reconnaissance Department (SRD), Major Richard Cardew, at 1st Army Headquarters, Lae. This immediately presented Major Cardew with a problem. All his reconnaissance teams were heavily committed to both the Sixth and Seventh Division to assist in preparations for the invasion of Wewak and Borneo. Now with an additional patrol required, no amount of juggling the schedule or shuffling personnel between teams would provide the additional manpower he needed.

Requests for assistance to the SRD headquarters in Brisbane came back with the suggestion to create a new team using men who had just finished or were about to finish their Z Special training. However, this suggestion met with some concerns by Cardew's staff. Even experienced operatives required time to settle in with each other—but these men had never been on an SRD mission before. With clandestine operations it was essential to know how other team members react to situations, and while they'd all be veterans of the New Guinea or Middle East campaigns, expecting them to become a cohesive team in a few days was unrealistic.

For the Muschu operation there would be no time for extensive preliminary training. The mission had to be underway by early April, when both tide and moon favoured a night insertion. The night of 12 April was selected as the target date as there would be no moon, disguising the team in its clandestine approach to the island from the sea. That gave barely a month to bring together all personnel, brief them, conduct rehearsals, then make a final reconnaissance before the actual insertion. Not nearly enough time in Major Cardew's opinion.

■ ■ ■

On 12 March, Major Cardew flew to Aitape to speak with the staff of the Sixth Division about the proposed Muschu operation and other patrols scheduled for the Wewak area. The intelligence summary during that meeting again noted that Muschu Island was now of 'some concern' due to the latest assessment indicating that the Japanese had brought their guns back into action. There was still conjecture about the island's role in the defence of Wewak, and the G3 Intelligence highlighted their belief that the island's garrison had been depleted rather than increased.

One alternative that had been considered was to bomb the island—not the small raids previously carried out by RAAF Beauforts and Bostons, but a large-scale 'pasting', European style. By 1945 the Australian Air Force had a large inventory of B-24 Liberator heavy bombers, and theoretically had more than enough to level the entire island. However, requests made by the Sixth Division had been refused by the Air Force's Operational Command in Australia as there was a shortage of 500- and 1000-pound bombs. Essential munitions were being rationed due to General Douglas MacArthur, Commander South-West Pacific, diverting stocks to support his operations further north. An ongoing dock dispute in Australia was delaying shipment of what munitions remained to New Guinea and therefore the Air Force was reluctant to squander what few large bombs they had on speculative targets. They needed a definite target location before they would schedule even a small raid by heavy bombers—let alone the squadron or more that was estimated as the minimum required to provide enough coverage to destroy a gun battery in heavy jungle.

So there was no alternative. The matter had to be dealt with using resources on hand, which meant risking men's lives in an operation that might have been unnecessary if enough bombs were available. It was especially frustrating given that the Americans, meanwhile, had the luxury of throwing such bombs lavishly around elsewhere in the Pacific.

Major Cardew was reluctant to deny the Sixth Division its request, recognising that if Muschu was to play a part in the defence of Wewak it was best to determine its role as soon as possible. The argument also had another aspect. After all, intelligence staff reasoned, Muschu was only a 'soft' target, garrisoned by an agricultural unit made up of recuperating sick, wounded and others classified unfit for combat duty. Also, being a reconnaissance mission lasting no longer than 48 hours, the patrol wasn't expected to make contact with the enemy—just get in, observe, then get out and report. Almost a training exercise.

Cardew wasn't convinced it would be that simple. However, Muschu had originally been scheduled along with a series of other operations around the Wewak area, and much of the planning had already been done. Codenamed 'Ash' at the time, it had then been decided to use eight men in the operation, including two officers, so that after landing, if it was deemed necessary, the patrol could be split into two sections that would then cover different areas of the island to save time.

Although the specifics would need updating, the basic format of the mission could remain the same. A patrol of eight would be inserted at night by kayaks onto one of the beaches, then proceed to ascertain the enemy's strength and preparations to defend the island. After completing their mission—and perhaps snatching a Japanese prisoner if the opportunity arose—they'd withdraw by kayak to be picked up by an Australian Navy patrol boat.

Finally, after hours of discussion and examination of the latest intelligence, Cardew agreed to supply a team to carry out the Muschu reconnaissance. The operation was given a new codename—'Operation Copper'—and was tentatively scheduled to commence on the night of 11 April, which coincided with the new moon—a 'black as the inside of a cow's guts' type of night that should make it almost impossible for the enemy to sight the approaching team.

Cardew wrapped up his discussions and flew back to Lae that afternoon in a Beaufort, passing high over Muschu Island during the flight. A smudge of green on a sparkling ocean, it looked strangely inviting.

7. 1ST AUSTRALIAN ARMY HQ, LAE:

13 MARCH 1945

On his return from Aitape, Major Cardew's staff began selecting men to take part in the Muschu operation. With twelve Z Special Unit training camps scattered around Australia, it was a drawn-out process contacting all units, gathering their assessments of potential candidates, then creating a short list—all conducted using the military communications system, which although now a large and efficient network, still suffered the limitations of the era. Messages needed to be encrypted, transmitted, then decrypted, while copying documents required additional time in the absence of modern photocopiers. Telephone conversations had to be scheduled over long distances, and line encryption used. Even internal phone calls needed to be carefully worded to minimise the possibility of compromise. All these factors added to the time and workload of preparation.

Had it only been merely a matter of selecting eight good soldiers plus a few reserves, the process would have been simple enough. However, besides being superb soldiers, each man had to be a specialist in such fields as explosives, radio, weapons or boat handling. All had to be cross-trained to some extent, and already at peak fitness as there wasn't time for the operational work-up associated with most missions. It took seven days to create a short list and another two days to make the final selections.

Those chosen for Operation Copper were Lieutenant Thomas Barnes, Lieutenant Alan Gubbay, Sergeant Max Weber, Lance Corporal Spencer Walklate, Signaller Michael Hagger, Signaller John Chandler, Private Ron Eagleton and Sapper Edward Thomas (Mick) Dennis. There were also two reserves nominated for the mission, both of whom were already in Lae. The team members were then interviewed by their unit commanders, told that they'd been selected for their first mission, then given three days pre-embarkation leave before being flown to New Guinea—all of them, that is, except one.

Sapper Mick Dennis was a former commando who'd seen extensive action in New Guinea in the opening days of the Kokoda campaign. No stranger to jungle warfare, Dennis had vowed to make life as miserable as possible for the enemy, managed to do so and yet possessed a lucky streak. In early March 1945, Mick Dennis had just finished his final Z Special course at the Tabragalba training camp south of Brisbane. Transferred to the holding unit at Milton to await embarkation to New Guinea, on 26 March he was ordered to pack his kit and report to the transport office where a vehicle would be waiting to take him to the docks. He was told he was being sent to join his new Z Special unit in New Guinea, and for him the prospect of a few days at sea was a pleasant one. What he didn't know was that he'd been assigned the three-day sea passage instead of a four-hour flight, due to an administrative foul-up.

Services Reconnaissance Department (SRD) staff discovered the mistake too late to have Dennis put ashore. This meant that by the time he arrived in Port Moresby and was then flown to Lae, he'd lose three, possibly four, day's work-up with the new team. In light of this, an administration officer at 1st Army HQ Lae suggested Dennis be replaced by one of the team's reserve members. The administration officer, a lieutenant who'd recently arrived on staff, claimed that Dennis's record showed he was an undisciplined larrikin who had little respect for authority and should never have been chosen in the first place.

SRD was reluctant to replace Dennis. Although losing three or four days' work-up training with the Muschu team was less than ideal, they'd been impressed by Dennis's service record. Dennis, 25, was five foot ten, broad shouldered, had a deceptively gentle manner, and came from a sporting family—one of his three sisters was a gold-medal swimmer in the 1932 Olympics. An unarmed combat instructor for the New South Wales police force before the war, he'd served in the militia since he was old enough to join, and after the outbreak of war was transferred to the Australian Imperial Force.

In 1941, Dennis volunteered for a new unit, the 2/5th Commando Company. In March 1942 the 2/5th was sent to New Guinea, where they fought the Japanese in a long guerilla campaign around Wau and Mubo. There, outnumbered almost a hundred to one, 'Kanga Force', as it became known, harried the Japanese for over a year, instituting a raid on Heath's Plantation in June 1942 that had been used ever since as a textbook example of commando tactics. Dennis had been cited for bravery under fire, carried wounded to safety, and shown initiative and leadership in this campaign.

He also had a reputation as a prankster, always up to mischief with one or more of his mates. A favourite pastime was playing with explosives—Dennis boasted he was so precise he could do anything with C4 explosives, from blowing up bridges to extracting teeth. Those who doubted him soon learned otherwise: it was amazing where explosives could be detonated at the most embarrassing of moments without damaging the human body.

While his pranks infuriated some, they provided the light relief so essential during times of hardship, diverting soldiers from their misery. The saying around the 2/5th was that if they really wanted to stop the Japs in New Guinea, all they'd have to do was hand Mick Dennis over to the enemy.

In 1943, the 2/5th returned to Australia for recuperative leave. During this period, out of boredom, Dennis volunteered for a series of training courses that eventually led him to joining Z Special in late 1944.

Even with his larrikin streak and disdain for authority, Dennis had been considered for promotion several times. He'd always refused, explaining that his purpose was to inflict pain on the enemy, survive the war then get back to civilian life. Promotion wasn't going to speed up that process—besides, if he did get promoted he'd wind up at a desk and that was something he feared even more than the Japanese.

■ ■ ■

Major Cardew's staff knew of Dennis's reputation and ignored the administration officer's suggestion, only to find that the officer had run the objection further up the chain of command. The SRD made its own decisions about its personnel—if it judged a soldier suitable that was it, irrespective of his conduct sheet. Even so, questions were asked about the wisdom of including Dennis in the squad, all quickly parried. However, the administration officer's enthusiasm to have Dennis removed had piqued the SRD staff's curiosity. Some quick investigating revealed that it was this particular officer who'd caused the transport problem in the first place.

While on pre-embarkation leave in Sydney 12 months earlier, the lieutenant had come across Mick Dennis in uniform in the Australia Hotel, standing at the bar with two gorgeous women giving him their undivided attention. The lieutenant, of the opinion that such lovelies would do better to lift their social standing by associating with an officer rather than a simple private soldier, attempted to muscle in by pulling rank.

Dennis merely burst out laughing and told the lieutenant to get lost. This inflamed the newly commissioned Duntroon graduate, who then proceeded to dress Dennis down in front of his escorts and an amused crowd of drinkers. Again, Dennis ignored him, then decided to visit the men's room without replying.

The lieutenant took this as a backdown and closed in on the two women, who now turned their attention to him. Encouraged further when they both accepted his offer of buying drinks, he began his sales pitch. He didn't get far when one of the women, the taller of the two, a slim and athletic brunette, moved seductively closer to him, smiled sweetly, then delivered a knee to his groin. Amid cheers from the onlookers, the lieutenant was then seized by a tall man wearing a fedora and grey suit, put in an arm lock, then hustled from the hotel and tossed in the back of a police car. The car sped away, siren blaring, and the lieutenant spent the night in the CIB cells at Central. In the morning, shackled to a hefty constable, he was delivered to Victoria Barracks somewhat worse for wear.

The next day the story got around. Lieutenant so and so was dropped by a woman, so how would he fare against the Japs? The lieutenant attempted to lay charges against Dennis, his female companions and the police for wrongful detention but found that he couldn't locate a single witness. What he didn't know was that the two women were Mick Dennis's sisters—and the one who'd felled him was none other than Clare Dennis, the former Olympic swimming gold medallist who was now married to a Sydney police detective who'd been watching from further along the bar. This detective had organised the lieutenant's transport and also made sure that all witnesses to the incident evaporated.

All this occurred without Dennis's knowledge. When he returned to the bar, his sisters made no mention of the incident and he assumed they'd given the lieutenant the brush-off. However, the lieutenant had borne a grudge against Mick Dennis ever since, and recognising his name in the administrative instructions being passed through Lae HQ, tried to interfere. There was no place for such animosity in an operational theatre: later that day, the lieutenant suddenly found himself boarding a C-47 headed back to Australia, to serve out the remainder of the war behind a desk.

8. Z SPECIAL UNIT, AITAPE:

27 MARCH 1945

While Mick Dennis was *en route* to Port Moresby by ship, the other seven members of the Muschu team were flown to Aitape. There they were given an initial briefing by the SRD staff on the enemy situation around Wewak, concentrating on the coastal areas north and south of the port. This briefing was a general outline only; there was no specific mention of Muschu Island for security reasons. In the interim, all they were told was that they'd be making a reconnaissance patrol somewhere around Wewak in early April. Meanwhile they'd prepare their equipment, carry out some preliminary training and learn to work together as a team.

The Z Special Unit detachment was situated near the beach about 4 kilometres from Sixth Division HQ. Using materials scrounged from the engineer's stores, successive occupants had built huts where they lived and worked in relative comfort. Here, patrols could train away from prying eyes and observation by other units that inevitably led to talk around the base. While the risk of a security leak was minimal, it was preferable not to tempt fate, as any hint to the Japanese of a new commando mission being prepared could result in them heightening security.

Vital to the mission were collapsible two-man kayaks known as 'foldboats' to be used for insertion and extraction. Four metres long, with a clip-together plywood frame covered by a pull-on rubberised canvas skin, they were designed to be quickly broken down into a compact bundle for transport or concealment. The same type of kayaks were used in the successful 1943 Jaywick operation into Singapore Harbour and they could carry a load of almost 100 kilograms plus two occupants. They differed slightly from the models the team members had trained on in Australia, but it didn't take long for them to adapt: by the end of the first day they were able to assemble, launch and handle the foldboats with ease.

Each boat would carry a two-horsepower outboard motor, wrapped in a waterproof sheet and carried in the stern compartment until needed. Although very quiet in operation the motors were intended to help only in escaping the island, not for the landing. They were checked and run, refuelled then packed away.

The team's radio men, signallers Hagger and Chandler, tested the equipment to be used on the mission. The main radios would be two ATR4 sets—high-frequency portable transceivers designed for long-range communications and often used by coastwatchers. The ATR4's vacuum tube construction was bulky by modern standards, weighing 11 kilograms complete with batteries. Their voice and Morse capability would be used to establish a base station and communicate with landing craft, or even communicate as far as Aitape if atmospheric conditions allowed. Hagger and Chandler confirmed both sets were operating and that the batteries were new, then packed them in their canvas haversacks and wrapped them in a rubberised canvas sheet.

In addition they had three SCR36 handy-talkies. Also known as walkie-talkies these short-range US Army handsets would allow the patrol to maintain communications if they had to split into two parties, and would also provide emergency communications with the Navy or reconnaissance aircraft. These too were tested, loaded with fresh batteries and wrapped in rubberised canvas.

For signalling their pick-up vessel, all men were issued with a torch. These were meant to be of a new waterproof design, but a dockworkers' strike in Australia had delayed their delivery, so they'd have to make do with the standard-issue item. Lieutenant Barnes raised the issue with the Aitape SRD detachment commander, noting that he had one of the new torches in his personal equipment, and suggested the commander should loan it to the Copper team. Although the commander declined, he ordered the quartermaster to send an urgent message to Divisional HQ, requesting the new torches be flown in. With over a week to go before the mission, there seemed to be plenty of time for SRD in Australia to obtain enough torches and put them on one of the daily flights to New Guinea from Darwin or Brisbane.

In the meantime, they'd have to train using the old torches. To improve their water resistance, the batteries and internal connectors were smeared with Vaseline, then the casing bound with electrical tape. Not perfect, but the best that could be done under the circumstances. They'd also carry two Verey signal pistols, along with an assortment of coloured flares and signal mirrors.

The main personal weapons for the mission were 9 mm Austen submachine guns, to which some team members objected. The Austen had a bad reputation: it had a habit of misfiring, or when it did fire, of 'running away'—continuing to fire even though the trigger was released. With a side-mounted magazine that snagged on foliage, it was awkward to wield in thick jungle, whereas the Australian-designed Owen gun overcame this drawback with a top-mounted magazine. The Austen also wasn't as rugged as the Owen, and not nearly as tolerant of dirt, mud or water.

Developed from the British Sten, the Austen was built in Australia (Australian Sten), and although it improved on the original design, with the wide availability of the Owen gun by 1945, its use by SRD was somewhat anachronistic.

Z Special's Austens, however, had been worked on by unit armourers, incorporating modifications that helped overcome many design weaknesses. All members of the patrol would carry Austens along with six spare magazines each holding 30 rounds. After being issued the Austens, the men spent a few hours on the range test firing and getting the feel of their weapon. As any soldier knows, each individual weapon, regardless of make, has its own personality. Trigger feel and pressure, recoil, accuracy—even the sound when the weapon is cocked—all add up to a unique character that soldiers recognise and which can only be gained through familiarity.

Accordingly, they were encouraged to practise whenever they could. Often Z Special members took this instruction literally and, being close to the beach, fired out to sea whenever the mood took them, much to the detriment of the local sea bird life which had become notably scarce in the area.

Each man would also carry a six-shot .38 calibre Smith & Wesson revolver with twelve additional rounds. Also divided among the team were four Welrod 9 mm silenced pistols. These were a British weapon that, unlike other pistols with add-on silencers, had the breach mechanism, barrel and silencer built as a single assembly. Using a specially designed subsonic round, with an effective range of 15 metres, the Welrod was reputedly the world's quietest assassination weapon, its only drawback being that it was a single-shot pistol and had to be manually reloaded from its six-round butt-grip magazine. To achieve silence, the round was propelled by a smaller charge than those used in the Austen or Owen gun, hence the Welrod's hitting power was reduced. Even the powder used was specially formulated to be smokeless and as near odourless as possible. All Welrods were test fired, cleaned, then reassembled. Those carrying them would wear them in a shoulder holster under the left arm.

Every man was also issued with a bush knife, a machete used mainly for hacking through jungle foliage—however, some team members sharpened both sides of the blade and ground it to a stabbing point, making it useful in close combat. Also available were a variety of killing knives, garrottes and other weapons, depending on personal preference. The principle was if you wanted it, you could have it, but you had to carry it.

Each man would also carry a water bottle and one day's rations—mainly chocolates, concentrated glucose tablets, a compressed fruit bar and hard biscuits. The plan was to be out for two days at most, so food wasn't a priority. In their personal kits they'd also have a compass, wristwatch and maps, water-purifying tablets plus a small first aid kit.

Mk 34 'Mills Bomb' hand grenades were issued and the seven men insisted on testing their batch of grenades to ensure they worked. To do this they trooped down to the beach and proceeded to hurl them off one of the ricketty palm-log jetties. The grenades functioned as advertised, the result being a harvest of fish that floated to the surface to be served that night in an impromptu tropical feast along with sake, beer and four bottles of Scotch that had been acquired from the Australian Air Force's officer's mess at Tadji airfield by one of the more larcenous members of the patrol.

The SRD commander turned a blind eye to the complaints that inevitably followed the next day, knowing that morale was proportional to his men's disrespect for authority. However, as a reminder of who was in command, he decreed that if they insisted on engaging in such behaviour then next time they should do it without leaving witnesses to the crime. To drive home the message he then sent all seven on a supervised pack run of 10 kilometres around Tadji airfield. They did it in under an hour.

For the next five days the team trained together around the Aitape area, practising weapons handling, field craft, concealment and foldboat handling—including assembling and dismantling the craft in darkness.

It wasn't until 5 April that the eighth man, Sapper Mick Dennis, joined the team. He'd arrived in Port Moresby and been flown to Lae, where he'd been put aboard an Australian Navy harbour defence motor launch—or HDML—to Aitape. Of wooden construction, about 24 metres in length, HDMLs were a British design adapted for Pacific operations, and were often used by the SRD. Powered by twin diesels, giving them a top speed of about 15 knots, carrying an assortment of armament—including two .50 calibre Browning machine guns and an Oerlikon 20 mm cannon mounted forward—they were versatile and rugged craft. This particular vessel, HDML 1321, had been assigned to the Muschu mission and was skippered by a former plantation owner, Naval Lieutenant Ernie Palmer.

Twenty-nine years old, Palmer knew the waters around the New Guinea coast well and, along with his crew of ten, had gained a reputation for an eagerness to pursue the enemy. During the voyage from Lae to Aitape, Palmer and his men went out of their way to ensure Dennis was made comfortable—they'd developed a special affinity with the men of Z Special and regarded them as their own.

Dennis came ashore in the morning and met the other members of the patrol. For the next three days they trained together, with Dennis quickly making friends and becoming part of the team. He found he had a particular affinity with 'Spence' Walklate, who'd been a constable in the Sydney police force before the war. Walklate had also been a St George first-grade rugby league forward and had played in the 1943 grand final against Dennis's home team and won. This sparked a friendly rivalry between the two men and they took every opportunity to outdo each other in training.

To the SRD staff, the team appeared to be coming together better than expected and their reservations about the hasty nature of the mission's preparation were somewhat relieved. Accordingly at 1600 hours on 8 April, after completing an afternoon's training in their foldboats, the team was called to the SRD briefing room—a small corrugated iron hut surrounded with sandbags.

They immediately knew something was in the wind: for the first time there were armed military police guarding all approaches and entrances to the Z Special area. As they shuffled into their seats in front of the lectern they noticed that the maps had been changed and there was a new display of aerial photographs.

The Officer Commanding then announced what they'd been waiting to hear: the mission was on.

The date: the night of 11 April.

Their objective: Muschu Island.

9. SRD BRIEFING ROOM, AITAPE:

8 APRIL 1945

Briefing soldiers about to embark on any mission—particularly one infiltrating enemy territory—is always a delicate balance between revealing information essential for the success of the operation and withholding other information as a precaution in the event of capture. In World War II torture was used by the Japanese as a normal interrogation method and despite popular perceptions—particularly by the Americans—that only the weak gave in under torture, it was widely recognised that no man could be expected to withhold information indefinitely when subjected to the variety of torture techniques used by the enemy.

SRD staff were acutely aware of this. Despite the established protocols of war, the Japanese insisted that Australian reconnaissance teams be treated as spies and therefore could be executed without trial—usually preceded by a long period of torture to extract the last essence of information from the unfortunate subject. So when briefing reconnaissance teams for any operation these facts had to be considered. SRD's Operation Order dated 10 April 1945 doesn't elaborate on the justification for the mission but instead laid out the essential information in a format and sequence that was the standard for the day—and has remained relatively unchanged within the Australian Army ever since. What the official records didn't show, however, were the points expanded on by the briefing officers.

One of the main factors for the renewed interest in Muschu Island—the status of the guns on the eastern high ground—was not included in the written Operation Order. The guns were, however, mentioned during the briefing and that it would be of value if their positions were confirmed. The fact that various intelligence agencies had pieced together a picture of the events before and after the guns' sighting was not explained—to do so could compromise the sources of information, particularly the existence of the radio intercept and deciphering units. While it would be naive to suggest the Japanese didn't suspect that Allied Intelligence had such units in place, there was no point in risking giving them evidence as to the full extent of the Allied capability by revealing to the patrol anything other than the most essential information.

Nor was the imminent invasion of Wewak mentioned. It was obvious to all patrol members what was going on around Aitape, with troops being trained and supplies being stockpiled. It may have been 'inspirational' for the patrol to know that this was all about to happen, but as this information wasn't critical to the mission's success it was withheld.

The men were shown the latest aerial photos of the island and known enemy positions, then told that during the next few days all patrol members would be taken on reconnaissance flights over the island so they could get a better appreciation of the terrain they'd be covering. The enemy was known to have built defensive positions on the western, southern and eastern sectors, with the bulk of forces thought to be in the western sector. Intelligence had assessed that the beach between Sup Point and Cape Saum was clear of enemy and was therefore selected as the patrol's insertion point. Much of this information had been gleaned from extensive aerial reconnaissance and captured records—information the Japanese were aware was already in Australia's possession, and therefore would be of no value if revealed during interrogation. However, the fact that there'd been recent movement to and from the island, mainly at night, was not explained, as it could compromise the presence of coastwatchers and native informants.

What the patrol *were* told was that the main garrison on the island consisted of second-line troops numbering about 300 to 400 and that this number may have been reduced as the fittest were being moved to reinforce the Wewak garrison. No doubt the knowledge that they'd be up against what could be unkindly described as a 'bunch of geriatrics and medical misfits' was of some reassurance, but all were acutely aware that one should never underestimate the enemy. The more experienced of the group knew this all too well, particularly Sapper Mick Dennis, whose previous combat experience in New Guinea had taught him that even dead Japanese could be dangerous. The enemy often booby-trapped their own casualties and he'd seen unsuspecting diggers wounded or killed as a result.

The patrol was warned to avoid contact with the locals on the island at all costs. While the Australian propaganda of the time portrayed all the New Guinea natives as smiling 'Fuzzy Wuzzie Angels' sympathetic to the cause and despising the Japanese, this was far from true. In reality, many of the locals had never seen a white man before and really weren't concerned about who won or lost the war. All they wanted to do was live their lives without interference, and their allegiances went to whoever was going to cause them the least grief. On Muschu, the inhabitants had been living side by side with the Japanese for over two years and had learned to coexist, even to the extent that the Japanese had established a school and a hospital on the island. To expect these people to suddenly switch sides by merely waving the Australian flag was naive in the extreme. So the men were ordered to stay away from the islanders, but if discovered by them, not to trust them—and if necessary, use the Welrod.

The aim of the mission was simply stated in the original SRD Operation Order:

Intention:

To insert a party on Muschu Island to,

Capture an enemy prisoner for 6 Div interrogation, and

To make a recce of the beach 800 yds NE of Cape Warbu.

The execution of the operation was relatively simple—on paper. On the night of 11 April, the team would be taken to Muschu onboard HDML 1321, then dropped in foldboats about 6 kilometres south-east of Cape Barabar on the southern side of the island. The moon would be in total darkness and the weather was predicted to be favourable, with clear skies during the day and perhaps some rain squalls in the late afternoon or early evening.

From the drop-off point, the team would paddle into the beach area between Cape Saum and Sup Point, lay up until dawn, then move further inland and create a concealed base position. From there they'd carry out the reconnaissance as required, either splitting into two groups or working as one team, depending on the situation. On completion they'd signal HDML 1321, either by radio or torch, make rendezvous at night and be back in Aitape for breakfast. The mission duration was expected to be 48 hours maximum.

In the event of a problem, HDML 1321 would wait out to sea during the day, moving in after dark to a rendezvous point about 4 kilometres off shore to await light, flare or radio signals. HDML 1321 could also give fire support from its Oerlikon and machine guns and send in a boat to pick up the patrol if help was needed. Tactical Reconnaissance aircraft would be making regular sweeps of the island and would be listening on radio and watching for light signals for several days after mission insertion in the event of loss of contact with the patrol. Listening watch on high-frequency would also be constantly maintained by the HDML and the SRD at Lae and Aitape.

If for some reason the patrol couldn't rendezvous with the HDML, it was suggested that they use the outboards and head to the mainland. The nearest Australian forces were at Dagua, about 40 kilometres north-west of Wewak. They'd be able to motor and paddle the distance in about eight hours. Tactical Reconnaissance aircraft would be patrolling the strait between the island and the mainland and would be able to provide cover until a pick-up was arranged. Light signals or radio could be used to contact the aircraft.

Radio call signs for the mission were 'X-Ray' for the Operation Copper patrol, and 'Boxer' for HDML 1321.

By the end of the briefing, there was an air of confidence within the team: this appeared to be a relatively simple operation. There was no reason to believe the enemy would be in a heightened state of readiness, most of the Japanese soldiers were second-rate troops and, from the aerial photos and description of the island, the landing area was easily defined—plus there was plenty of cover to conceal the patrol once on shore.

Their confidence was further boosted by a report that another patrol, codenamed 'Oregon', had gone into Cape Moem just east of Wewak during the night of 7 April with the intention of capturing a prisoner, yet despite this being an area reported to be crawling with Japanese, they'd returned empty-handed without even sighting the enemy. The natural competitiveness between teams only made the Muschu patrol even more determined to succeed.

To conclude, the briefing officer introduced the Medical Officer. A tall, lean captain with a thin smile, the MO proceeded to remind the team about the importance of malarial precautions and other matters of field hygiene, adding as a postscript: 'And for those of you who have them, don't forget to check under the foreskin for leeches.'

After a few moments of chuckling and friendly banter, the young men noticed that the MO had taken on a more serious stance. He waited until silence returned, then without saying a word produced a large wooden cigar box from his haversack. This he opened and from it distributed eight small metal tins with hinged lids, warning the team not to open them until he said to do so.

On command, holding them carefully upright as instructed by the MO, they opened the tins. Inside each one, packed in protective foam rubber, was a tiny glass phial.

'Cyanide,' he announced flatly. 'Simply place in the mouth and bite.'

There was silence as realisation set in. These were suicide pills.

During training, all the men had been made fully aware of the treatment they could expect if captured by the Japanese, even to the extent of attending a 'code of conduct' course where elements of physical and psychological torment were experienced first hand. But suddenly being given the means of self-destruction in such an innocent-looking form had a powerful impact on all. For a long moment the silence hung heavy.

Then suddenly someone spoke up.

'Jeez Doc, guess if we take one then we don't need to come and see you in the morning, eh?'

Everyone, including the MO, dissolved into laughter. After a few minutes composure was regained, and after a quick question-and-answer session the patrol was dismissed. They had two days to make final preparations and now that they knew exactly what would be involved, there was plenty to do.

What the men hadn't been told was the fate of an earlier Z Special mission that had until recently been assumed lost. Gathered by radio intercept and local agents, Special Operations Executive information indicated that ten men from Operation Rimau—a mission into Singapore Harbour to sink Japanese shipping, based on the successful Jaywick operation of 1943—were now being held in a Singapore prison, where they were being brutally tortured almost daily.

10. AITAPE HARBOUR:

11 APRIL 1945

It was a clear, sunny day, with a light breeze ruffling the water. At 1100 hours, HDML 1321, with the men of Operation Copper on board, slipped its moorings and headed out of Aitape Harbour. Passing through lines of landing craft and freighters, the patrol returned the waves of crews who paused to watch the little ship motor past. While the mission itself was secret, there were many who knew that the Navy's HDMLs worked with the 'Z Special blokes' and to see one pass by loaded with determined-looking men dressed in jungle green and wearing berets could only mean another Z Special operation was underway.

Once clear of the port the commander, Lieutenant Palmer, gave the order and the diesels were throttled up. HDML 1321 set course east, slicing through the long swell at 12 knots in an easy, comfortable motion. Palmer intended keeping well offshore until they sighted Vokeo Island, then using the island as a navigation marker, turning east and approaching Muschu after dark—the somewhat roundabout route chosen to remain clear of observation from both Muschu and Kairiru Island. It would take about eight hours to reach Vokeo, and from there another three to four hours to reach the drop-off point.

The team's foldboats were lashed to the deck on both sides of the ship and covered by canvas. Most of the equipment had already been stowed aboard the foldboats, so there was little for the patrol to do to pass the time. A few busied themselves by cleaning their Austens and rechecking their personal gear, but one could only occupy so much time in these tasks and after the first few hours, most of them were stretched out on the deck trying to sleep. Even that proved difficult for some, the combination of nerves and the ship's motion keeping them awake, several of them becoming seasick.

The time before any mission is always testing, even for the most seasoned veteran. It takes a tough mental attitude to prepare for the dangers that lie ahead and no amount of training can completely allay the nagging fears that inevitably enter one's mind before the action begins. The worst enemy at these times is inactivity, and soldiers will always find a way to divert their attention. Be it a game of cards, swapping stories or writing letters, all become diversions to stop them dwelling on their fears. Ironically, as many soldiers will explain, often that fear isn't about their own safety or survival, but how their death will affect their family or loved ones. Many of the letters from that era reflect this and during HDML 1321's run to Vokeo Island, several of the patrol took the opportunity to write a final letter and entrust it to the crew who'd agreed to ensure it would be delivered if they didn't return. This would be done via a network of couriers—soldiers, sailors or airmen going on leave who would circumvent the mail censorship regulations to make sure that parents, wives or lovers received word without interference or delay. It was a practice the military found they couldn't stop, despite threats of the harshest punishment.

Those first hours of the voyage were particularly surreal for some of the Muschu team. As one of the ship's crew later described it:

> The day was a perfect one, the soft rumble of the diesels, the easy motion of the boat through the blue water gave the impression that we were out for a pleasure cruise. Occasionally a wave broke over the bow sending spray high into the air to fall back over us in a fine mist. There were even flying fish that launched themselves off our bow wave then fell on the deck flapping and wriggling until they dropped over the side. It was times like these that it was hard to believe we were at war.

At 1740 hours Vokeo Island was sighted. Lieutenant Palmer's navigation and timing had been perfect and he ordered speed reduced to 3 knots, while maintaining their heading towards the island. After dark he'd alter course and head in towards Muschu to position the patrol for insertion, but for now, in the off-chance they were under observation, they'd give the impression that they were heading towards Vokeo.

Before last light the crew served up a meal of hot tea and corned beef sandwiches—after that the patrol would have to rely on their ration packs. Most ate heartily, spirits buoyed by the prospect of action, minds now focusing on the job ahead. Their final preparation was to 'cam up'—blacken faces and exposed skin. As the boot polish was applied, during the application someone began a rendition of Al Jolsen's 'Mammy', which although quickly ended by a curt order from one of the officers, shattered the tension that had been building for hours.

In the tropics, once the sun has set, darkness swiftly follows. That evening the sunset was a vivid display of gold and orange against a clear sky, with high clouds in the west over the mainland flickering with lightning. As the last glimmer of sun faded, HDML 1321 swung round onto a south-westerly heading. Throttling up to full speed, the ship passed on a safe course through a minefield south of Kairiru Island, then headed towards the eastern coast of Muschu. At 2230 hours, Palmer calculated they were in position 6 kilometres south-east of the island and throttled back until the boat was barely making headway.

The night was pitch black, the only light coming from the backdrop of stars. Just the vaguest silhouette of Muschu could be discerned with the naked eye, a blackness that disrupted the line of the horizon where the stars met the sea. They could feel and smell the island rather than see it. Quickly, the patrol made ready. First over the side were the foldboats. Then two men per kayak slipped on board the tiny craft. A final equipment check, then amid whispered farewells and good wishes from the crew, they shoved off to be quickly lost from view. The departure time recorded in the ship's log was 2315 hours.

HDML 1321 remained on station for another two hours in the event of the team making a sudden return. On hearing nothing and knowing that the kayaks should have reached the shore within an hour and half, they set about and powered away from the island to a position out of sight where they would spend the daylight hours waiting. There they sent a quick Morse transmission by HF radio back to Aitape.

SL, SL, SL.

Mission inserted.

■ ■ ■

The Muschu team had been paddling for over an hour, the four kayaks keeping close together in the darkness. In the lead foldboat were Lieutenants Barnes and Gubbay, followed by Hagger and Eagleton. Further back were Dennis and Chandler, with Walklate and Weber paddling a few metres behind. It was just under 6 kilometres from the drop-off to their landing point on the beach between Cape Saum and Sup Point. This they'd estimated would take them about an hour and a half; however, it was now obvious that the current was stronger than expected, and was pushing them well south of their objective. Although the mission timings had been calculated to coincide with high tide when the currents were minimal, lack of knowledge of this remote area was working against them as the tide swirled around the island in unpredictable patterns.

In the lead foldboat, Lieutenant Barnes raised his paddle over his head, a sign for all boats to close on him. This they did and he ordered everyone to pick up the pace. Adjusting course to allow for the current, they increased their stroke rate. But although they were superbly fit and their training had often seen them paddle continually for six hours at a time, the exertion was beginning to take its toll. To maintain headway they had to paddle at a higher rate than normal and it was becoming a test of endurance befitting any Olympic champion.

Barnes knew that if they hadn't reached shore by 0200 hours they'd have no choice but to turn about, paddle with the current as far as they could, then signal the HDML to pick them up before dawn. Even that would involve considerable risk as they'd probably be in a position about 2 kilometres out, right beneath the guns on the eastern end of the island. They'd soon find out if the guns were serviceable or not at that range.

After another half-hour it seemed that the current was easing. Muschu now loomed ahead, a black mass against a curtain of stars. They pushed on, moving faster as the current's effect lessened in the lee of the island. In the last foldboat Mick Dennis felt a sudden change in the sea's motion. He stopped paddling. Behind him Chandler also paused. Both of them could feel the swell running beneath the boat. The stern was lifting first and they immediately knew it meant the water was shallowing as the swell neared the shore. Suddenly ahead, they saw a line of surf breaking against a reef.

A wave swept past them and the lead foldboats vanished in a welter of spray.

Chandler and Dennis dug their paddles in, trying to stop their forward motion, but felt the suction of a wave building behind them. The stern lifted and both men leaned back to keep the bow from digging under as the boat surged forward. For 50 metres they ran straight, using their paddles to steer, but then the bow lifted as the water poured over the reef. They felt the boat rise, then suddenly slam down, the timber frames creaking as the wave washed over them. Somehow they remained upright, the boat surging ahead again. In the darkness it was impossible to see beyond the surrounding foam and all they could do was try and keep the boat straight.

They shot forward, and then ahead saw another line of white water. Helpless, they ploughed into the foam wall. For a moment they thought they were through, but the bow went under and they slewed sideways. Before they could react they'd capsized. Both men dug in their paddles, ready for the coordinated move to bring them upright, only to have their paddles ripped from their hands by the force of the wave. Then suddenly the foldboat shuddered to a halt.

In seconds both men were out of the boat, standing in water up to their armpits. Cursing softly they righted the boat and checked their equipment. All of it had been strapped in waterproof coverings inside the craft and apart from a drenching, seemed intact. Chandler had lost his Austen gun and he futilely groped for it in the darkness, but soon gave up.

The waves had dropped, most of their power dissipated by the reef. With the boat stern-on to the waves it was now manageable, all they had to do was to wade inshore—yet when they tried moving they were gripped by something spongy and resilient that blocked their passage. It was soft coral, long strands that grew up to the surface, creating a forest through which they had to fight their way. They were exposed and vulnerable, not knowing what lay ahead. Where were the others? Had they run into the Japanese? The only reassurance was that they hadn't heard any gunfire, yet that meant little—perhaps the Japanese were waiting for them all to reach the beach. But there was no alternative, they had to go forward.

It took an exhausting hour to swim and push the foldboat ashore. There they found that the rest of the team had met a similar fate. Quickly and in silence they concealed the foldboats among the palms lining the beach, then hid nearby. They realised that they'd missed their objective and were on the beach on the western side of Cape Barabar, an area suspected to be regularly patrolled by the Japanese. However, there was nothing they could do until morning. Checking their weapons they formed themselves into a defensive circle and waited.

11. MUSCHU ISLAND:

12 APRIL, 0600 HOURS

Corporal Buzuki was looking forward to breakfast. He and his section of eight men had been awake all night on guard duty, gazing over a black sea under an even blacker sky. They'd manned an observation post on a high point at the western end of the island overlooking the strait between Muschu and the mainland and this was the fifth night he'd been given this duty. He knew it was important work, but the sheer boredom of it was mind numbing and it had become an endurance test for all.

Although they were grateful for the relative comfort of a large palm-log bunker that had the luxury of mosquito netting to keep out the swarms of insects that descended after dark, it was a real problem keeping everyone awake. Soldiers had the most amazing ability to fall asleep, yet at a glance appear alert at their post, and his men were no exception. In some ways he was glad of the diversion from the ceaseless scanning of the ocean, for it allowed him to play a little game of let's see who I can catch dozing.

That night he'd caught all of them napping. He'd feigned outrage at their dereliction of duty, but everyone knew it was mainly bluff, for he too had been caught nodding off several times. It was annoying, for there had been word of Australian commandos landing on the mainland almost directly opposite them and they'd been ordered to stay alert for any signs of a boat, submarine or whatever craft the commandos might be using to bring them near to shore.

At first the excitement of the possibility of contact with the enemy had kept them all alert, but the inevitable boredom set in and they'd succumbed sometime after midnight. Buzuki had woken first, checked his watch and realised he'd dozed for almost twenty minutes. He woke up just in time to make the half-hourly report by field telephone back to the command post—a procedure that ensured the night watch remained alert or warned of something amiss if the call wasn't made.

So when daylight came and the phone jangled to announce that the relief section was on its way, Buzuki breathed silent thanks to whatever god protected soldiers who had to remain alert all night for attacks that never came. He also sent thanks that no enemy had landed when they were asleep at their posts and crept up on them and slit their throats.

He was looking forward to the rest of the day. After a breakfast of sago and bananas, he'd sleep until noon. Then he'd eat again—unlike the garrison ashore they had plenty of food, for the surrounding waters were rich in sea life. Tonight he wasn't on duty, so he could afford to remain awake, perhaps wander over to the naval artillery unit where they had a short-wave radio that could pick up Tokyo.

It was just after 0600 hours when the relief section arrived. After exchanging brief formalities, Buzuki and his men trudged off east along the track towards their base camp, rifles slung over their shoulders. A hundred metres on, the track branched towards the beach. Buzuki decided that as it was now low tide they'd take the beach diversion as this provided an opportunity for them to search for sea life that may have been stranded during the night.

They reached the beach after a quick walk. The tide was low, leaving rockpools and dips in the sand. One of his men whooped in delight: in one rockpool was a large crayfish, which he promptly skewered with his bayonet and held up, its spindly limbs flailing and sending drops of water sparkling in the morning sun. Buzuki grinned as they found more crayfish, heaping them in a flapping pile on the beach. Quickly they gathered vines to bundle the spiny crustaceans together.

Buzuki looked back along the palm-fringed beach. It was protected by a reef about a hundred metres out, forming a shallow, clear lagoon. In happier times, this would be regarded as a tropical paradise, and for him in some ways it was. Tonight they'd dine in style—one crayfish was more than a meal for any man, and they'd found over a dozen. Being the ranking non-commissioned officer he could take two of them and trade them for a bottle of sake—a precious commodity of which there was a surprising quantity both here and on the mainland, if one knew who to trade with.

He was about to turn around and rejoin his men when something on the beach caught his eye. Near the high-water mark was an oval shape partly concealed by weed—a turtle perhaps? That would indeed be a bonus, for turtle meat and eggs were regarded as delicacies. As he approached he realised that it was no turtle, but a canoe paddle—probably lost by one of the island's inhabitants. He paused two metres away. It was double-ended and painted black. This was no rough-hewn paddle, but one of modern design—and it looked new. He felt the hairs on the back of his neck begin to tingle.

Quickly he glanced about. This could mean only one thing: commandos had tried to land along the coast and had hit the reef. Had they drowned? Or were they nearby watching? There was no indication that anyone else was on the beach, for the sand in both directions had been smoothed by the withdrawing tide.

For a moment his main fear was that the commandos had come ashore while he and his men had been asleep. However, he quickly reasoned that if the commandos were nearby they would have retrieved the paddle to prevent it being discovered and compromising their presence. So the chances were it had been lost further east and drifted in with the current on the rising tide.

Unslinging his rifle, he called to his men, ordering them to take up concealed positions watching the beach and for one to return promptly to the command post and report the finding.

The time: 0615 hours.

12. MUSCHU ISLAND:

12 APRIL, 0630 HOURS

The eight men of Operation Copper spent the remainder of the first night cold and shivering, with two awake at all times while the others tried to rest. Most had suffered coral cuts when they waded to shore and these now ached, making sleep difficult.

At the first greying of dawn, all woke and lay with weapons ready, seeing their surroundings for the first time. They were in high grass among palm trees and vegetation that became dense jungle further inland and from which now came the raucous screeching of waking birds. Behind them the beach was a wide strip of smooth, empty sand, the drag marks and footprints from their landing the previous evening erased by the tide. Waves were breaking on the exposed reef in a muffled roar and the sun shimmered off the lagoon. Beyond the lagoon, a flock of gulls were noisily circling and diving into a school of fish that was moving west along the coast. The scene was deceptively peaceful.

For half an hour they lay watching for any sign of the Japanese, their senses becoming attuned to the island. The air warmed quickly and a light breeze ruffled the palms while the bird calls eased to a steady background noise of hoots and whistles. As the sun climbed higher they were able to make out in detail the low hills to the east that would be their first objective. Finally, after almost an hour with no sign of the Japanese, they quickly moved their foldboats 30 metres into the tree line, then again went to ground and waited.

After satisfying themselves that they hadn't been observed, they unloaded the foldboats, covered them with foliage, then moved all their equipment further inland to an area of thick scrub about 100 metres from the beach. While the rest of the team lay on guard around them, the signallers unwrapped the two ATR4 transceivers to find they'd been soaked through. However, as the radios were internally coated with protective wax, the signallers agreed that little harm would have been done and the radios would dry out in the heat of the day. They unplugged the batteries to prevent internal shorting, then covered the radios with the waterproof canvas sheet and concealed them beneath palm fronds. They discovered that one of the walkie-talkies had been lost, and that the remaining two handsets had also received a drenching. They drained them and hid them near the ATR4 sets to dry.

Lieutenant Barnes then called the group together to review their situation. Considering the problems they'd had crossing the reef, they were in good shape. No one had sustained serious injuries and the coral cuts were more a nuisance than anything else—antiseptic cream from their medical kits should prevent any infection. They'd lost some equipment, including two paddles, two Austen guns, one walkie-talkie, a spare radio battery and some Verey flare cartridges, but this wasn't enough to render the patrol ineffective. Those who'd lost their Austens still had their Smith & Wessons and they were given a Welrod each as a backup.

There was some discussion about whether the lost equipment would be found by the Japanese; however, all agreed that as it went overboard on the reef well out from shore the chances of anyone finding it were slim. All of it would have sunk, except for the paddles, which were designed to float. But as they'd been lost on the reef, they would have been wedged in the coral far from view or even swept back out to sea. A quick check along the beach confirmed they hadn't washed ashore nearby.

It was decided that the mission would continue. Although they'd missed their landing point and were now further west than planned, they should be able to reach their initial objective in an hour. Their present location provided good cover, so it was agreed this would become their primary lay-up area and rendezvous if they became separated. When the radios dried out they'd set them up, but as they were only to be used for calling for an emergency extraction they weren't essential. HDML 1321 would return to their original drop-off position, which would now become the rendezvous for their extraction.

Again Lieutenant Barnes went through the procedures for the mission, including alternative rendezvous points, light signals for the torches, mirrors and Verey flares. They then checked their maps to ensure everyone was correctly oriented. Also every man was to record information in their patrol notebooks, the duplication being a precaution if they separated or were captured or killed, to maximise the chances of at least one patrol member getting the information out.

After Barnes finished his briefing, all weapons were cleaned and oiled, the men working in pairs—one cleaning his weapon, while the other stood watch. They then ate a quick meal from their rations, then doublechecked the area to ensure all equipment was concealed and that they'd left no signs of their presence. Then they moved off, heading east through the scrub towards Sup Point.

After about half an hour they found a track that headed north. Cut through dense foliage, the track looked well used and they were at first reluctant to follow it, but if they stayed off the tracks, the dense foliage would slow their movement to such an extent that it would take hours to cover distances that could otherwise be travelled in minutes. So they spread out, spaced themselves alternately on either side of the track, then moved on.

Ten minutes later the track steepened as it climbed towards Sup Point, where they found a series of defensive positions built along the top of the ridge. On the highest point about 20 metres above the beach was a bunker made from heavy timber and coral rock, with a view commanding the beaches to the north and to the south-west. Shaking out into an assault line, they quickly closed on the bunker but found it unoccupied. Covered by the others, Mick Dennis climbed inside to find it clean and tidy, but otherwise unoccupied. From its dominating position and all the phone cables that were dangling inside, they assumed it was an observation post for directing the defences in this area. Dennis used his compass, took a bearing to the southern tip of Kairiru Island and noted it on his map.

Looking west from the operation post, about 500 metres out, Chandler pointed out a false crest in the hill. Behind it, among tall trees, beneath the heavy jungle canopy, they could just make out what looked like a gun emplacement. Using his binoculars Lieutenant Barnes scanned the area and confirmed that there was definitely something there—it looked like a camouflaged gun position dug into the side of the hill. The movement of the trees in the wind cast changing shadows that made it difficult to see exactly what it was, but the position coincided with the suspected gun location reported by divisional intelligence, so it was likely that this was it. The false crest hid the emplacement from the sea, while the thick overhead cover concealed it from aerial observation. Only when the rising sun cast light into the area was the emplacement visible to an observer from a low angle, which explained the difficulties Sixth Division Intelligence had been having trying to locate it. He marked his map and suggested that if they had time later they would reconnoitre the area further.

Also visible from the bunker was an L-shaped slit trench running west then north along the clifftop to Cape Saum almost a kilometre away. There were bunkers spaced at 50-metre intervals along the trench, so again the patrol shook out into an assault line and advanced on the first bunker, only to find it was also unoccupied. However, inside was a medium machine gun—a 7.7 mm Juki or 'woodpecker'. The weapon was in good condition and had only recently been oiled. They dismantled it and tossed the components and ammunition into the sea.

The patrol then moved further along the trench line to the next bunker, where another Juki in similar condition was found. This was also dismantled and thrown over the cliff. They continued examining all the bunkers and when they reached the northern end of the defences at Cape Saum, they'd found and destroyed four machine guns.

They now realised how lucky they'd been. The defences overlooked their original landing area and the shoreline provided very little cover. From the condition of the weapons in the bunkers, it looked as if they were manned at night and the chances were they would have been sighted as soon as they reached shore. Being caught in arcs of fire from four Jukis, they'd have stood little chance of surviving.

The fact that there were no sentries posted there during the day indicated that the Japanese regarded these defences as of secondary importance. Not far away would be a base encampment from which troops could be called on quickly. If they could find that base area it would help the Air Force later, and possibly also provide an opportunity to snatch a prisoner.

There was a network of paths behind the defences leading inland to the west, and they decided to follow what looked like the main trail. Moving silently, after fifteen minutes they came to a large clearing filled with tilled vegetable gardens and about a dozen thatched huts spread around the perimeter. The area appeared to be deserted, so they waited five minutes then moved in. Working as two groups, one covering the other, they checked each building and after finding them all empty, moved further on to a stretch of higher ground 50 metres away that had been cleared of foliage. From there they could see the mainland and the port of Wewak.

After taking more bearings so the position could later be accurately fixed on the map, they moved away from the clearing, found a well-concealed area among the trees and called a halt. Comparing notes, they concluded that the defences at this end of the island were probably only kept in a state of readiness rather than being continually manned. This fitted with the Sixth Division Intelligence's assessment that the island garrison was being stripped of the fittest men to reinforce the mainland defenders.

The meticulous layout of the gardens meant they were Japanese owned, as the islanders never bothered with such precision. There were also several species of plants that were only favoured by the Japanese, and the healthy condition of all the crops indicated they were regularly tended. The location of the huts in the tree line and their thatched construction was probably deliberate, to help conceal them from aerial photography and to give the impression that they belonged to the islanders. None of the patrol could recall having seen the clearing when they'd flown over the island on the preliminary reconnaissance, which reinforced just how simple it was to conceal anything from the air in jungle areas.

For a few minutes there was speculation about how easy the patrol had been. It was now just after 0800 hours, they'd been on the island less than twelve hours and despite their original setback, had accomplished a major portion of the mission. They were surprised by the extensive track network—like a 'ruddy bloodshot eyeball' someone remarked—but this was only to be expected after almost three years of occupation. Of the Japanese there'd been no sign, which was unexpected, but it was likely that they'd be found further west in the coastal area around Muschu Bay, where they were known to have living quarters and more food-production areas.

It seemed the Japanese here were less than vigilant, which also tended to confirm intelligence assessments of the garrison's quality. Lieutenant Barnes reminded everyone that this was no reason to be less cautious, however it did make them more confident in using the tracks rather than forcing their way through the undergrowth. He also cautioned that as they moved west, the chances of making contact with the enemy would increase.

They decided the best course of action would be to return to their equipment cache near the beach. There the signallers could check the radios and after a rest and a quick feed, the patrol would head west towards Muschu Bay in search of a prisoner. All were confident they could finish the reconnaissance by the end of the day, and if they found a suitable prisoner they'd be able to leave the island after nightfall and make the rendezvous with HDML 1321. That would mean they'd completed the mission in less than 24 hours—something of a record, Lieutenant Barnes suggested.

After a weapons check, they set out. Quickly skirting the empty huts they located and followed what they thought was the track that had brought them in.

Unfortunately it wasn't.

13. MUSCHU BAY:

12 APRIL, 0800 HOURS

Captain Tomei of the Japanese Imperial Navy was the commander of Muschu's base force or Tokubetsu Konkyochitai, located near Muschu Bay at the western end of the island. Two days after the Japanese captured Wewak in 1942, a small detachment of marines landed on the island and claimed it for the Emperor. Since then, despite the Japanese Army being in overall command of the area, Muschu remained under naval administration. In practical terms it made little difference who was in command, as Tomei received his orders from the 8th Army's headquarters in Wewak and he obeyed them irrespective of the cut of his uniform. His job was to ensure the island produced food and palm oil—and as long as he produced the goods he was left very much alone.

At this Tomei had been very successful. An intelligent man in his late forties, he'd enlisted the support of the islanders and, using a carefully balanced mixture of stick and carrot, persuaded them to cooperate. Under his stewardship, Muschu had become an important production area and his men, a small cadre of marines supported by about 300 assorted Army troops, lived a relatively comfortable existence, despite regular interference by the Australian Air Force—some of the Japanese soldiers even taking local women for wives and producing children.

In early April 1945, after more than two years commanding the island, Tomei was informed that he was to return to Rabaul at the end of the month, where he would await reassignment. His successor was Captain Temura, a former destroyer commander whose ship had been sunk in the Battle of Leyte Gulf in October 1944. Wounded in action, Temura spent six months recuperating, then rather than accept the pension offered to him, had persuaded the Navy to give him another command. Instead of another ship they suggested Muschu Island. For some reason best known to himself, Temura swallowed his pride and accepted. Determined to erase the shame of losing his ship, he'd arrived on Muschu boasting he'd increase production and turn its garrison of misfits into a fighting unit the Emperor would be proud of.

Tomei ignored his bravado, expecting that after a few weeks on Muschu, reality would set in. However, Temura proved obstinate from the moment he set foot on the island. For a week prior to assuming command, accompanied by his aide, he prowled his new domain making notes and finding fault in almost everything he saw. For the official handover of command on the morning of 12 April, Temura insisted on gathering the entire garrison to the headquarters area to witness his formal acceptance of office and the raising of his personal standard.

Tomei cautioned that this meant losing a day's work in several of the outlying gardens that were being harvested, and that withdrawing patrols from the coastal areas would compromise security. Having more than 300 personnel gathered in one place could prove an inviting target for any Australian aircraft that just happened to be passing at the time.

Temura ignored the advice, insisting the ceremony take place early in the morning and that increased vigilance by observer teams would give adequate warning of any approaching aircraft. And so it was that at 0700 hours, with the sun shafting through the palm trees, the garrison paraded on a hastily cleared grass square between the thatched bamboo huts of the headquarters. Standing on the covered porch of the hut to one side of Temura, Captain Tomei couldn't help seeing the pathos of the moment. Here was a man who firmly believed a miracle would happen and Japan would be saved from the humiliating defeat that must soon befall it.

The troops stood awkwardly to attention as they listened to the lengthy harangue from their new leader. Finally, after almost half an hour of threats, promises and propaganda, Temura's pennant was raised to flutter limply in the sea breeze. They presented arms, dutifully shrieked 'Banzai' in a parody of a time now gone, then marched off to filter back to their units scattered around the island.

Temura, encouraged that Tomei's warning about marauding Australian aircraft had proven wrong, watched the men disperse, then strode into his office to begin his first day as commandant. What he didn't realise was that the Australian Air Force was under orders to avoid Muschu for the next two days—standard procedure for any area where an SRD patrol was operating. His insistence on maximum attendance had also left the door open for the men of Operation Copper and made their job of reconnoitering the eastern defences a relatively simple one.

So when he was greeted by an orderly who'd been impatiently waiting throughout the proceedings to convey an urgent message, he treated the man in a somewhat offhanded manner. The message was from a sentry post on the island's south-western coast, reporting that a section of men returning from overnight duty had found a canoe paddle on the beach.

At first Temura dismissed the information as irrelevant—there were, after all, hundreds of natives on the island and plenty of canoes. The orderly tried to explain further, but he was cut short by Temura. It was then that Captain Tomei, who'd been listening to the conversation, stepped in.

It took only a few questions for him to ascertain the situation. The paddle in question wasn't from a native canoe. It was of the type used by Australian commandos, and it was a clue that an attempt had possibly been made to land on the island. He pointed out the intelligence information received two days earlier indicating that Australian commandos had been sighted by natives in the Cape Wom area north of Wewak, which is why he'd insisted that guard posts on the western end of the island remain at full alert instead of being stripped to attend this morning's ceremony.

Temura seemed more annoyed that these personnel had missed his speech than concerned about the threat of a commando incursion, and it took all of Tomei's patience to control his anger. However, Tomei politely pointed out that until 20 minutes ago, he'd been in command of the island.

The argument that followed was later described in the diaries of one of the headquarter non-commissioned officers, who wrote that they were now in the hands of an egomaniac who seemed to be living in another world—the actual translation being 'came from another planet'. To the HQ staff listening in the orderly room, separated only by thatched walls, it sounded like a father lecturing a recalcitrant child, with Tomei speaking in low measured tones while Temura shrieked abuse, claiming that under Tomei's command the island had become a haven for misfits, and the only honourable thing Tomei could do to expunge such a disgraceful record was to commit *seppuku*.

After another half-hour's delay, Temura issued orders for the patrol on the beach to make a sweep further east to determine whether there were any more signs of the elusive commandos, ignoring Tomei's suggestion that he also put out a warning to all sub-units around the island. Temura wanted to wait until he had further information rather than send out false alarms within minutes of taking command.

At this Tomei merely shrugged, then told Temura that as he obviously didn't need any further assistance he would leave him to his own devices. Accompanied by his orderly, he headed for the little hut near the beach that was to be his quarters for the next few weeks until he flew to Rabaul.

14. MUSCHU ISLAND:

12 APRIL, 0900 HOURS

The Z Special patrol moved south-west expecting to come to the junction that would lead back to their equipment cache, but after fifteen minutes, they realised they were on the wrong track. The front man, Lieutenant Gubbay, suddenly propped, motioned for everyone to be quiet, then crouched down. Ahead was a deserted village—and in the clearing, only 20 metres away, he'd sighted a Japanese soldier. The soldier was standing scuffing the grass with his foot, head down as if searching for something. Gubbay signalled that they would take him.

Two of them remained concealed to protect the rear; the others moved quietly into position in a half-circle, then on Gubbay's signal broke cover and surrounded the soldier. Taken by surprise, he stared at the Australians, then slowly raised his hands over his head. Max Weber spoke to him in Chinese, which the Japanese evidently understood, explaining that the soldier was now their prisoner and would come with them. To drive home the point that the prisoner was not to offer any trouble, Weber made it quite clear that if he did so he'd be shot without warning. The soldier was then disarmed, his hands bound behind him and his mouth gagged.

His uniform insignia showed he was a private soldier first class, and his identity papers would later reveal his unit. He was young—about twenty—and looked fit and healthy. Lieutenant Gubbay remarked he didn't exactly look like the second-line soldiers that Sixth Division Intelligence believed comprised most of the island's garrison. Positioning the prisoner near the rear of the patrol, they then moved off. However, the prisoner suddenly decided that he wasn't going to cooperate and despite a shove in the back, stood his ground. Weber warned him again and aimed a Welrod at his chest. The prisoner stared sullenly back.

Spence Walklate broke the impasse by seizing him by the scruff of the neck and the seat of his pants, then lifting him bodily off the ground. Walklate, who'd been a policeman before the war, was a big man over six feet tall, and in his beefy hands the Japanese soldier looked like a child. For a moment the patrol's discipline was shattered as Walklate announced in a booming voice:

'I'm marching this bastard into Regent Street Station and charging him with being a bloody nuisance to humanity and resisting arrest.'

With the soldier's stubby legs pedalling the air, Walklate frogmarched him along the track, administering solid kicks to his rump with his size 12 boot every second pace. After 20 metres the prisoner decided that cooperation was the best course of action and dutifully behaved.

The patrol headed back up the track at a fast pace, intending to find the trail that would lead them to the equipment cache. At another junction they turned off towards the sea and followed a track that paralleled the beach. Believing they were still east of their cache they continued west, but after an hour realised they'd gone too far. The mainland was clearly visible and the island of Kairiru couldn't be seen, which indicated they'd gone a long way past their original landing point. Again they paused to take stock of their position.

One of the group scouted ahead about 50 metres, where he came to a small clearing near the beach. On its edge among the palm trees were two small huts. The area looked deserted, so he returned and reported his finding.

There was a quick discussion as to whether they should turn back now—after all, they had achieved the mission's primary aims. Even so, the absence of Japanese in any numbers seemed odd. Someone quipped that maybe it was a Japanese holiday, or that the war had ended during the night and they'd all gone home.

Lieutenant Barnes agreed there wasn't much point in going looking for the Japanese, but said they should check out the huts before turning back. Leaving two of the patrol to guard the prisoner, the patrol spread out and advanced on the first hut.

Suddenly, a Japanese soldier appeared at the door and ran for the bushes. Barnes shot him mid-stride with his Welrod, the soldier falling with hardly a sound face-down in the grass. After checking the body, they moved into the hut. Inside were two beds, a small cooking area and some fishing nets, but nothing to indicate that it was used for anything other than a rest area for off-duty personnel.

Moving outside, they closed on the second hut 20 metres away. Peering in, they saw it also had two beds. On one bed lay a Japanese soldier, wearing only his trousers, on his back asleep. Lieutenant Barnes and Gubbay quietly went in. The soldier suddenly woke and dashed for the door, but was felled by a headshot from Mike Hagger's Welrod. He dropped against the wall and slid to the floor. They checked his body, found some papers which possibly indicated his unit and identity, then made a quick search of the hut. Again nothing important was found.

After another quick discussion Lieutenant Barnes decided that it looked as if the huts were used as a recreation or rest area, possibly for local defences. If they could fix the huts' position the Air Force could deal with them later. So after sending one of the team back to fetch the others, the patrol moved off, still heading west.

Three hundred metres further along, the track opened onto the beach. Forming into a defensive position near the end of the track they observed the shoreline. The beach curved south towards a jungle-covered headland, marked on the map as Cape Warbu. The sun glistened off the lagoon, and the rising tide had already partially covered the reef, allowing small waves to reach the shore. A flock of gulls worked the water beyond the reef, squawking and diving. There were no signs of the Japanese, which again struck the patrol as strange.

In a central location overlooking the beaches on the southern side of the island, Cape Warbu was a logical area for defensive positions, so the decision was made to continue the reconnaissance onto the cape, then turn and follow the coast back to their equipment cache. There they would wait until nightfall, then paddle out to the rendezvous point and signal the HDML.

Everyone was in high spirits as the mission had gone better than expected. They had gathered valuable intelligence—one small but important piece of information being the network of tracks along the coast, which any landing force would need to mark carefully to avoid confusion.

They waited five minutes, then after assuring themselves the beach was deserted, they moved out, staying close to the tree line and widely spaced. All they had to do now was reconnoitre the cape, then another hour should see them safely back at their lay-up area.

15. MUSCHU ISLAND:

12 APRIL, 0915 HOURS

Corporal Buzuki's belly was making rumbling sounds he feared could be heard a hundred metres away. Patrolling the beach with four men spread out either side of him, he tried to keep his mind from wandering to thoughts of food. He was used to three meals a day and for him, missing breakfast was unheard of since his time with the infantry. Once slim and athletic, he was now overweight, his trousers and shirt stretched tight around his stomach. The wound that left him with a shattered left leg had long since healed, however a convenient limp and regular gifts of crayfish to the medical officer were enough to keep him on the island. But now as he trudged through the sand with sweat stinging his eyes, he wished he hadn't taken such a liking to sago or bananas.

His runner had returned after half an hour with orders to keep the beach area under observation until further instructions arrived. For the next two hours they'd sat concealed among the palm trees, watching the paddle on the sand as if expecting it to suddenly come to life and make a dash for freedom. When word eventually came from HQ, they were ordered to check for signs of any enemy landing along the coast to the east as far as Cape Warbu. Buzuki tried to conceal his displeasure—they'd already spent most of the night awake and he'd not eaten for almost fourteen hours. Now he and his men were expected to walk 5 kilometres or more in the blazing sun in search of an enemy they believed either didn't exist or had long since gone. As they approached Cape Warbu, rifles at the high port, he wished he had never sighted the paddle in the first place.

■ ■ ■

Nearing Warbu from the east, the Australian patrol passed beneath a cliff where they could see camouflaged machine gun positions, one of which appeared to be a 20 mm Oerlikon. There was no sign of the Japanese, so they moved on, then paused 20 metres from an outcrop of rock that had long ago tumbled from the cliff and spread across the beach. In the lead, Lieutenant Gubbay signalled everyone to take cover. As one, they moved off the sand into the tree line at the beach's edge and waited. Gubbay went forward 10 metres then froze. A few metres ahead atop a high boulder was a tripod-mounted heavy machine gun, aimed out to sea. From behind the boulder a Japanese soldier appeared. He stood looking at the lagoon then stretched sleepily, broke wind, then removed his shirt and sat down on the sand. For a moment all watched him as he sunned himself, then Gubbay signalled the patrol to move forward and make ready to take him prisoner.

The soldier lay oblivious to the patrol as they approached, weapons ready. Max Weber called to him in Chinese, but after opening his eyes and bolting upright, the soldier merely grunted and shook his head. A big man—almost six foot tall—he slowly stood then, jaw clenched, eyed his opponents as if searching for a weakness. Four of the patrol surrounded him and Weber repeated his question in Chinese, but again the soldier shook his head.

Lieutenant Barnes indicated he should put his shirt on and this he understood. Slowly he shrugged it on, then stood defiantly looking around him. The insignia on his sleeves indicated he was a sergeant in the Kaigun Rikusentai—the Japanese marines. As Z Special personnel wore neither badges of rank nor unit insignia when on patrol, it may have appeared that he'd been captured by soldiers of only private rank. Someone remarked that he looked 'very pissed off'—to be captured by soldiers of inferior rank was obviously a disgrace.

After checking the sergeant's pockets and finding identity papers in his wallet along with a photo of a woman and child, Weber bound his hands at his back. They hadn't expected to capture a second prisoner, but seeing this one was a marine non-commissioned officer they realised he could prove valuable.

Lieutenant Barnes ordered the machine gun destroyed and Sapper Dennis volunteered. He quickly climbed up to it, dismantled the gun and threw its components into the sea. To ensure it wouldn't function even if the parts were found, he damaged the heavy recoil springs by hammering them with a rock. As he climbed down from the gun position, he noticed a thatched shelter behind the boulder. Quickly, his Sten gun ready, he checked the shelter and found six hammocks, all recently used.

He returned to the patrol and told Lieutenant Barnes, who agreed they appeared to be near a major defensive position and that perhaps they'd be pushing their luck to continue further. With an extra prisoner on their hands it would be too difficult to move quietly, so it was time to get back to their lay-up and wait until night. Dennis was ordered to take charge of the new prisoner, then the patrol shook out and moved off.

As soon as the patrol began moving, the Japanese sergeant sat down and refused to budge despite a hefty prod by Dennis. To emphasise the point, Dennis drew his Welrod and pressed it to the man's head. Still he refused to move. Dennis called to Barnes, suggesting that the only way to make the marine sergeant comply would be to carry him slung on a pole between two men like a trussed pig.

Barnes shook his head, ordered Dennis to shoot the sergeant if he continued to refuse, then moved off.

Pressing the Welrod to the man's temple, Dennis repeated his order. It was obvious the marine sergeant understood its meaning and the consequences, but he merely grunted, stayed sitting, jaw clenched and refused to budge.

So Dennis squeezed the trigger. The weapon misfired.

The sergeant remained motionless, staring ahead. Dennis re-cocked the Welrod, put it to the man's head and repeated the order. Again he grunted and refused to move.

Again Dennis squeezed the trigger. Again the pistol misfired. He cocked it but this time it was obvious the firing-pin spring was broken, so he hurled it out into deep water then, without warning, flicked off his Sten's safety catch and put a single round in the sergeant's brain. The dead man crumpled forward onto his face, a pool of blood spreading from the wound onto the sand. Dennis left him and caught up with the patrol.

They now headed inland from Cape Warbu, intending to pick up one of the tracks that ran parallel to the coast. By now they were becoming used to the deceptive maze of trails that crisscrossed the island and were careful to remember identifying features each time they came across one. After about 20 minutes of moving through heavily wooded jungle they found telephone cables strung low between the trees running north-south. Eager to put as much distance as possible between themselves and the Japanese that would undoubtedly be at either end of the lines, they turned ninety degrees to the cable direction and continued, a compass bearing confirming they were headed north-east.

Movement was slow through the heavy undergrowth. After two hours they came to a track they recognised as the one leading to the deserted village at the eastern end of the island where they'd originally captured their prisoner. Continuing on and skirting the village, they found the track that led to the bunkers along the clifftop between Cape Saum and Sup Point. From there it was a simple matter of identifying the trail that led back to the lay-up position. Relieved that they'd finally found the right track, they rested for ten minutes then started back towards their kayaks.

16. MUSCHU ISLAND:

12 APRIL, 1100 HOURS

On the beach half a kilometre west of Cape Warbu, Corporal Buzuki signalled a halt. He'd heard something that sounded like a muffled shot, but it was too faint for him to be sure. In the waters off to his right, beyond the reef, a flock of gulls wheeled and squawked as they dived on a school of fish, so he decided he'd confused the sound with their shrieks. Looking at the others, he cupped a hand to his ear with a questioning expression, only to receive shrugs and raised eyebrows. None of them had heard anything, so he put it down to his imagination. Tired, thirsty and hungry, all he wanted to do was finish the patrol, satisfy his grumbling stomach, then flop on his cot for the rest of the day.

Wiping the sweat from his brow, he signalled the patrol to move on. With resigned looks they obeyed, one of them cursing loudly as a small wave swept up the beach and splashed over his boots. The sun was high now and their small peaked caps provided little protection. The water in the lagoon was rising with the tide and looked cool and inviting. Buzuki tried to concentrate, but found his mind wandering to thoughts of home, his children and better times.

Fifty metres from the tumble of rocks at the base of the cliff, Buzuki paused again. By now they should have been challenged from the command bunker high on the cliff. But then he remembered that the entire marine platoon assigned to this area had been withdrawn to attend the ceremonial parade. Even so, there should still be *someone* on watch.

He'd been to this area many times, as he'd made friends with the sergeant in command. Sergeant Hiroto and his men were experts at distilling a potent brew from coconuts and spices, which he traded for sake three to one. Buzuki knew that although Hiroto's men were at this morning's ceremonial parade, Hiroto had refused to attend, citing the proceedings as a waste of time and insisting that someone had to remain to keep watch. Only a stubborn old veteran like Hiroto could get away with such insolence, and Buzuki expected to see him sitting on the boulder at the base of the cliff with his faithful Juki. Most mornings, Hiroto would engage in target practice with the weapon, popping off streams of tracer into the gull flocks feeding on the fish that came in with the tide. But this morning he wasn't there—nor was his Juki.

He went forward cautiously, then 10 metres from the fallen boulder he froze. Hiroto was lying face down on the beach, his head encircled by bloody sand. The muffled gunshot had been real after all.

Buzuki snapped orders to the patrol. They fanned out and took cover among the rocks while Buzuki checked the body. Carefully, almost as if approaching a sleeping loved one, he knelt beside Hiroto. Buzuki saw that his hands were bound, and felt an anger he hadn't experienced for a long time. Slowly he rolled the dead marine onto his back. Hiroto's eyes were still open, his jaw set in a determined expression that Buzuki had seen many times before when he told of his experiences in the early days of the war. Barely containing his rage, he ordered one of his men to go to the shelter behind the rock and bring a blanket to cover the body.

Buzuki then carefully examined the area. The body was surrounded by a maze of boot prints in the hard sand, leading to and from a track that emerged from the tree line east of the cape. He gauged that perhaps ten or more men had passed through here, undoubtedly Australian commandos from the pattern of their boot prints. As they'd made no attempt to hide Hiroto's body, Buzuki concluded they were an assassination squad intent on terrorising the garrison with random killings. They'd been warned about how the Australians were using death squads to sow fear among the defenders on the mainland, and how they often cut off their victim's ears or penis for trophies. Stories had spread about how most of them were selected from felons held in Australian prisons, murderous thugs descended from British and Irish convicts who were promised a pardon if they killed a Japanese soldier. They were rumoured to be huge men, trained in the crudest methods of killing and torture, with no concept of honour or code—white barbarians who were little more than animals.

Suddenly Buzuki forgot his hunger. From the tracks in the sand he reasoned that the Australians were heading east, possibly towards Sup Point. He ordered one of his men to take the cliff trail up to the command bunker and use its field telephone to report the situation and advise headquarters he was pursuing the enemy.

■ ■ ■

Following the track back to their lay-up, the Australians came to the abandoned village where they'd captured their first prisoner. Lieutenant Barnes was in the lead and suddenly propped and gave the caution signal. In the clearing ahead were three Japanese soldiers. One of the soldiers called out a name and at the rear of the team, the prisoner lunged forward. Walklate seized him by the collar, dragged him back and rammed his Welrod into his stomach, shaking his head. The prisoner glared at him, tried to call out but only managed muffled grunts against his gag. Walklate shoved his Welrod behind the soldier's ear and clicked back the hammer. The prisoner immediately quietened.

The Japanese kept calling, and Barnes indicated that they should bypass the clearing and head south. They left the track, pushing quickly through the dense undergrowth until they came to the beach. Scrambling down a steep incline onto the sand, they moved west in single file for another 400 metres then, calculating they were past the Japanese, began climbing back up the slope. In the rear the prisoner tried to climb, but despite forward shoves by Walklate, kept falling. Seeing the problem, his hands were untied, then bound again in front of him. This allowed him to climb slowly.

After the patrol reached the top, they quickly found the track again. For a moment they waited, making sure they'd left the Japanese well behind. Satisfied, they spread out and prepared to move off.

Suddenly Japanese voices were heard further up the track. Before anyone could stop him the prisoner whipped his bound hands up to his gag, tore it down and screamed a warning. Walklate slammed the butt of his Welrod over his head, knocking him to the ground, but he rolled away and kept yelling. Ron Eagleton drew his Welrod and shot him in the head.

The Japanese rushed around the bend and came face to face with the Australians. Startled by the sight of eight big men, who in the dim light of the jungle must have looked like spectres from a kabuki play with their blackened faces, the Japanese fled into the jungle.

Barnes gave the signal and the patrol broke track and headed south again towards the beach. As they moved they discussed what they should do; the consensus was that they should get off the island as soon as possible. Now that the Japanese were alerted they couldn't risk trying to capture another prisoner and it was vital the information they had was returned. Fortunately, the sea was now calm and they wouldn't have to fight waves breaking on the reef. If it remained calm they could risk setting out after last light; if not, they'd have to wait for high tide, which would be just after midnight. Once over the reef they could use the outboard motors to quickly reach the rendezvous, then signal the HDML with torches.

With luck, they'd be back at Aitape in time for a late breakfast.

17. MUSCHU ISLAND:

12 APRIL, 1300 HOURS

Corporal Buzuki's patrol moved steadily along the beach, heading east towards Cape Barabar. It was past midday and the sun was now on his back, giving some relief from the glare off the water. His mouth was dry and he'd already drained his small water flask, yet thirst wasn't important—he could drink later. With the tide now at its lowest, the beach was almost 20 metres wide and he'd spread his men in an extended line across the sand. He kept glancing over his shoulder, searching for the runner he'd sent to report Sergeant Hiroto's murder, but he suspected the soldier wasn't very enthusiastic about rejoining the patrol. He couldn't blame him. Several times Buzuki had questioned himself on the wisdom of pursuing what was probably a force superior in number and skill to his men, yet the answer always remained the same: it was his duty to do so.

So they trudged on, the coral sand squeaking beneath their boots, nerves tingling at the knowledge that at any moment they might come under fire. It was times like these Buzuki hated, the vulnerability of being out in the open and the thought that someone ahead was taking aim. He'd made sure his section was well separated in a V-shaped formation, which made it difficult for a single shot or burst of automatic fire to hit more than one man from the front or the flanks. The problem always was though, who would that man be? He could only hope that when the time came everyone remembered their battle drills.

Putting these thoughts aside, Buzuki surveyed the beach ahead. Here the jungle thinned to high grass and palms in a broad fringe that extended almost 50 metres to the sand.

They had gone almost 2 kilometres past Cape Warbu when one of his men, walking close to where the grass met the beach, suddenly halted and called out in a loud voice. Buzuki turned to him, wanting to rebuke him for breaking voice discipline, but realised that in his excitement the man had forgotten everything he'd ever learned about infantry work. He was pointing agitatedly at the sand, then into the undergrowth, fear written on his face.

Buzuki waved the patrol into extended line and advanced them to the edge of the undergrowth to take up firing positions protecting the flanks and inland. Only then did he trudge over to see what had drawn the soldier's attention.

In the thin strip of soft white sand above the high-tide mark was a series of faint grooves that indicated something had been dragged from the beach into the undergrowth. An attempt had been made to brush them out, but the traces of two grooves remained. Buzuki complimented the soldier on his find, then gave the command for everyone to advance in extended line either side of him, searching ahead as they went. He also gave the order 'safeties off', which meant every man was to carry his rifle safety catch released, ready to fire.

Slowly they advanced into the undergrowth, pushing through the high grass towards the jungle. After about 50 metres, the man on Buzuki's right called out. Again he ordered everyone to pause, take cover and stay alert.

Then he strode over to look at the find. At the base of a tall palm tree, covered by fallen branches, were four kayaks. He smiled. So this is where the Australians had landed.

Carefully he walked around the kayaks, making sure there were no trip wires or booby traps. Then he ventured a look inside one, checking the front compartment to find a paddle identical to the one he'd found on the beach. The rear compartment also held a paddle and behind the seat was an outboard motor wrapped in canvas.

Now he was faced with a dilemma. Should he continue the search or should he wait here? Was this the only landing point? The four kayaks could hold eight men, but because of the maze of footprints he'd seen in the area where Sergeant Hiroto was murdered, he was convinced there were more in the raiding party. He decided to despatch another runner to the nearest command post, about a kilometre inland. All his men knew the island's track system well and it would take less than ten minutes for the runner to get there and raise the alarm. Meanwhile he would search the strip of undergrowth for a hundred metres either side of the kayak-hide for signs of more commandos. Then they would remain here and await further orders.

■ ■ ■

Captain Temura was becoming increasingly frustrated. A message had come in from an outpost reporting that a sergeant had been found shot dead near the Cape Warbu defences, and there were more signs that Australian commandos were loose on his island. His immediate reaction was that this would look bad on his record—he'd been in command less than four hours and already the enemy was making a mockery of his security. Maintaining a stern face, he strode into the little room that served as an operations centre and examined the map. An orderly had marked the place where the paddle had been found with a neatly flagged red pin and was now marking the location of the dead sergeant with another.

Temura's first order was to alert all outposts and have them deploy as many men as possible to the western half of the island. This should have been a simple procedure as the field telephone network extended to all units; however, as he quickly learned, raising the alarm wasn't as simple as it first appeared. His insistence on having all garrison troops attend his ceremonial parade had left several key posts unmanned, and with most of the troops returning on foot it would be hours before these were manned again. He sent runners to catch up with those now *en route* to turn them around and bring them back.

Half an hour later he received a report from the eastern area near Cape Barabar that three soldiers from a harvesting squad had come face to face with a large group of Australian commandos on a track near the coast. They'd described how they barely escaped the barrage of fire laid down by the commandos by deploying into the cover of the jungle. After assessing the situation, they told how they'd then started out in pursuit of the Australians only to find the body of one of their comrades. They called off the chase and reported in.

Then a few minutes later came a report from the central coast area that two more soldiers had been found shot dead. This was soon followed by more reports—the defences between Sup Point and Cape Saum had been sabotaged, with four machine guns destroyed and possible booby traps laid.

Temura broke out in a cold sweat as he watched the orderly jab more pins into the map. He'd never commanded ground forces before, and this situation was beyond his training. The closest experience he could liken it to were damage-control exercises at naval college where ship compartments were flooded using a model simulator, and which usually ended with the model turning belly up or sinking—Temura had the uneasy feeling that if he didn't get a grip on this situation very quickly, the same thing would happen to his career.

From the welter of reports flooding in, it was obvious to him that a large commando force had landed. They were working in two—possibly three—groups of twelve or more, concentrating on the western, central and eastern areas. Having ordered his forces to concentrate on the western sector, he now needed to redeploy them to ensure all sectors were covered. The result was significant confusion as Temura despatched more runners countermanding his original orders.

Temura began to panic as the field telephones began an almost constant jangling and the map became crammed with more red pins. Was this an invasion?

During the commotion, Captain Tomei was kept well informed: his staff remained loyal even though protocol demanded they now obey Temura. At first Tomei was amused by the idea of messengers scampering all over the island and troops dashing about chasing shadows, but when he was passed news of Sergeant Hiroto's death he was furious. The old sergeant was a friend who'd been through several campaigns with him and deserved better than execution at the hands of assassins. Putting on his uniform, he buckled on his *katana* sword, then strode up to the headquarters and took command.

Temura was livid, but there was nothing he could do. His staff simply ignored him and obeyed Tomei, knowing that in time of emergency he had the right to assume command. The legalities of the situation could be worked out later, but now the immediate priority was to determine exactly what was happening.

Quickly Tomei assessed the situation, then sent a squad to reinforce Corporal Buzuki's patrol guarding the kayaks, ordering him to take charge, remain in his location and set an ambush. He knew that eventually the

Australians would try to leave the island and they'd need their boats to do so.

Then he ordered that a message be sent to the mainland advising them of the situation. Depending on what happened in the next few hours, he might need to call on their reserve company to assist with hunting the commandos down. To this Temura objected strongly: to call for assistance was a sign of incompetence, an admission of weakness.

Tomei ignored him and the message was sent.

18. MUSCHU ISLAND:
12 APRIL, 1500 HOURS

Fifty metres east of their foldboat hide the Australians paused. They were in heavy undergrowth, with Lieutenant Barnes in the lead. He stopped and signalled everyone to go to ground, indicating he could hear voices ahead. Moving slowly forward until he could see along the beach, he peered through the grass to glimpse a group of twelve—possibly more—Japanese soldiers in the area where the boats were hidden. Two heavy machine guns were mounted on the beach covering the hide. Withdrawing carefully, he moved back to the others, signalling that the area was crawling with Japanese and indicated they should head inland and find a safe lay-up.

After travelling about 200 metres into the jungle, they found their equipment cache, picked up two of the radios, then continued on for another hundred metres. Satisfied they couldn't be overheard, with two of the patrol covering the direction they'd come in, they gathered together to discuss their situation.

The consensus wasn't good. It now looked as if the entire island was alerted. HDML 1321 would be at the rendezvous between Cape Warbu and

Cape Barabar during the night and without the foldboats they'd have no way to reach it. With the Japanese waiting, signalling the HDML for a beach pick-up wasn't practical. The boat would have to lay off the reef and send in a Zodiac. Even if the sea was calm, crossing the reef would be dangerous and then they'd still have the Japanese to confront. The HDML could of course lay down a significant barrage of covering fire, but in doing so it would become a prime target for the heavy machine guns and cannon on Warbu—not to mention the two large naval guns further east. Sitting off the reef less than a kilometre from shore, the HDML would be blown out of the water.

Sapper Dennis suggested they move further inland to higher ground and get a radio working. They could then set up an alternative rendezvous for the HDML, perhaps west of Cape Saum where there were no outposts and they could send in a boat to pick them up. The idea was agreed on by the two signallers, but rejected by the others as the Japanese would be listening out for any radio transmissions.

Dennis then proposed that they should sneak up on the Japanese, wipe out the gun crews and as many enemy soldiers as possible, then retrieve the foldboats and put to sea using the outboards. Once over the reef they should be safe. However, they were uncertain exactly how many soldiers were guarding the kayaks, and while they'd have the element of surprise on their side, a night attack without sufficient time for a thorough reconnaissance beforehand was very risky. They'd have to kill every soldier, because once they were in their boats, with no covering fire they'd be easy targets for anyone on shore until they crossed the reef. The idea was ruled out.

Another option was to use their torches to signal the HDML. They could do this from one of the headlands in relative safety as the HDML would be within torch range all night. This would need to be a one-way conversation, as any return signalling would not only reveal the HDML's position but could also compromise those on shore. However, the signallers had previously discussed this scenario with the ship's captain. There were other ways they could acknowledge receipt of light signals, including firing shots from their .50 calibre machine gun—one round for yes, two for no. The quick bursts of gunfire, without tracer, could be heard on shore, but their source would remain a mystery to the Japanese. After all, there was a war in progress and gunfire was fairly common in these parts. This option looked like a possibility, and using it they could set up an extraction from the northern shore. However, the idea was dismissed when an examination of the remaining torches found that all of them had leaked and their batteries shorted into useless lumps of soggy chemical.

Someone then suggested that they build a raft from driftwood then swim it out to sea. By morning they should be at least 5 kilometres out, and from there they could mirror-flash one of the Tactical Reconnaissance aircraft that were scheduled to reconnoitre the island and nearby waters during the day. They were briefed to look for signals if the patrol failed to make the night rendezvous and should easily see eight men on a raft.

Sapper Dennis, the strongest swimmer in the patrol, cautioned against the idea, warning that they'd be at the mercy of the currents, and even with eight of them paddling, getting out far enough was doubtful. The two signallers agreed and again argued for using one of the radios—either the ATR4, or the walkie-talkie. The walkie-talkie was probably the best option as it didn't need setting up, and being short range there was less chance of the Japanese listening in. Talking in veiled speech and using their pre-arranged codewords, any Japanese overhearing their transmission wouldn't have a clue what they were talking about. Once the rendezvous was agreed on they could quickly move to another location in case the Japanese did manage to fix the radio's position. But, as no one knew for certain whether the enemy had radio direction-finding equipment, the idea was again overruled.

They then voted on the raft-building option, and it was carried five to three. The area chosen for the attempt was the eastern tip of the island, at Cape Barabar. This was about 2 kilometres from where the Japanese were guarding the beach, and as the morning's reconnaissance had revealed that the nearest defences were on the northern side of the cape, they should be able to construct a raft and put to sea without being seen.

Feeling confident the plan would work, the patrol prepared their equipment, cleaned their weapons, then ate from their rations. The two signallers made a quick check and confirmed that the radios had dried out. Although they couldn't test them, they believed they would now work, so they carefully wrapped them in the waterproof sheet and hid them again. With two men on watch, they all took turns resting for the remainder of the afternoon. There were no further signs of the Japanese, so it looked as if the patrol weren't being searched for—at least not on this end of the island.

By late afternoon, all were awake and eager to get moving. They'd been on Muschu less than 24 hours, yet as someone remarked, this had been the longest day of their life.

At 1730 hours, just as the sun was starting to nudge the horizon, they set out for Cape Barabar.

19. EAST OF MUSCHU ISLAND:

12 APRIL, 1800 HOURS

During the day of 12 April, HDML 1321 cruised east of Muschu Island, out of sight over the horizon at a distance of approximately 16 kilometres. In the tiny wireless shack, the radio operators took shifts maintaining listening watch on the patrol's high-frequency band and by late afternoon, hearing nothing, it was assumed the mission was going as planned. Except for scheduled 'operations normal' reports back to Aitape consisting of two-letter Morse transmissions made at pre-arranged times on different frequencies, HDML 1321 had also maintained radio silence. They gave their last 'ops normal' at 1700 hours. Their next report would hopefully be a transmission to Aitape sometime after 2400 hours confirming pick-up of the Copper team.

At 1730 hours Lieutenant Palmer ordered a change in course. The little ship headed for the night rendezvous off Cape Warbu at a speed calculated to bring them close to the island by 2100 hours.

The mood on board was one of confidence, tempered by apprehension. They were, as Lieutenant Palmer reminded them, going right under the very noses of the Japanese and two naval guns, against which their cannon and machine guns would be as powerful as a 'fart against thunder'.

Sobered by this earthy yet strangely fitting comparison, they prepared the ship for action. While still out of sight of the island, the gun crews were called to their stations. The Oerlikon team loaded a drum of 20 mm onto their weapon and fired a three-round test while the two Browning .50 calibre crews broke out boxes of linked ammunition and tapped off quick bursts into the sea.

At 1821 hours night descended, a darkness so heavy one could almost reach out and grasp it. On deck the watch strained to make out the island against the horizon. In the aft cabin, one of the crew fetched a bottle of rum from a locker to make 'gunfire' coffee as a reward for the completion of a successful mission. Beside him another crewman spread out the medical kit in readiness. Just in case.

■ ■ ■

The men of Operation Copper reached Cape Barabar by 1830 hours. Using large pieces of driftwood and palm trunks that had been piled in the lee of the cape by the currents, they lashed together a crude raft using vines and rope from a fishing net found among the debris. Hauling it into the water they found it floated well and, although not capable of supporting their full weight, it was enough to act as a buoy for them all. After lashing their weapons and equipment to the raft, they pushed it out to deep water.

Stroking and kicking, the eight men held on and headed towards the open sea. There was a small break foaming across the reef and soon they were being swept by white water—uncomfortable for those not used to the surf, but manageable. In the dark it wasn't possible to see the approaching swell, and many of the waves slammed into the patrol without warning, causing several to lose their grip and become temporarily lost until they scrambled back to the raft again.

As the vines binding the logs became soaked, they stretched. The raft began to twist and bend. Still they pushed on, the waves getting steeper, coming in sets of four that pounded them under, then eased off for a minute, only to come at them again. For almost an hour it was two steps forward, one step back as they battled the rising swell. Then, hit by a big wave, one of the vines parted and their equipment broke loose. Dennis shouted to the team to sling their weapons around their necks but before they could do so another wave swept everything away.

For another two hours they fought to get beyond the break, several times paddling clear only to have large waves sweep them back. By this time the raft was a jumble of logs loosely held together by fracturing vines. Finally, after a hammering by three huge waves, the raft disintegrated and the eight men washed ashore clinging to the debris.

They struggled up the beach into the tree line and collapsed in exhaustion. All except Dennis had lost their Sten guns and packs. For an hour they rested, then moved further into the heavy undergrowth and found a lay-up position.

It was 2300 hours.

■ ■ ■

HDML 1321 arrived off the island at 2100 hours, then commenced cruising a racetrack pattern along the coast at 4 knots. Because the charts were inaccurate, Lieutenant Palmer was reluctant to come any closer than 2 miles, as at night it was impossible to determine the reef line. Even 2 miles offshore it was still possible to hit an uncharted rock or reef, so Palmer kept the speed down to a sedate pace. As a precaution against being heard, the ship's twin exhausts had been modified to muffle the engines and this was most effective at low speeds.

At 0100 hours hot tea was served to the watch and Lieutenant Palmer remarked to one of the crew that he was looking forward to the traditional rum-laced brew that would mark the mission's end. There was hearty agreement from those on deck—all had been on enough Z Special missions to know that unless they ran into unexpected problems, the 'Z blokes' were usually on time for the pick-up.

By 0200 hours they were becoming concerned, but not yet alarmed. This wasn't the first Z Special team to be late for their rendezvous and certainly wouldn't be the last. But worries were being voiced by the crew, and Palmer knew they had a collective sixth sense that was uncannily accurate.

If Z Special were in their foldboats heading for the rendezvous, they would have signalled by now. This meant they were probably still on the island. And that could only mean they had run into difficulty. Or did it? The lack of any signals—light or radio—could mean anything.

Another hour passed slowly. Still there were no light signals or radio messages. Again Palmer reminded the crew that the patrol had been scheduled to last a maximum of 48 hours and they probably just needed more time to complete the mission. He'd give them another hour, then withdraw and stand off over the horizon until it was time to return.

At 0500 hours Palmer gave the order and HDML 1321 went about and headed away from Muschu.

■ ■ ■

Resting in their new lay-up the patrol discussed their situation. With only a few hours left until daylight, if they didn't act now, they'd have to wait until the following evening. The Japanese now fully alerted, would probably begin a thorough search of the coastline and post sentries on all the high ground, which would make future escape attempts very difficult. All except Dennis had lost their automatic weapons, and with only Smith & Wesson revolvers and two Welrods, their firepower was no match for a Japanese squad. Someone light-heartedly suggested they could always go 'bush' and live off the land or steal from the enemy until the war ended, but all knew that this would be an absolute last resort. So it was vital they escaped from the island that night.

Lieutenant Barnes proposed they again try getting out to sea—this time using small logs as individual floats. Gubbay, Walklate and Eagleton agreed, but the rest were against the idea, particularly Dennis. He'd understood the power of the currents and believed they'd only be swept ashore further along the coast. Even if they did make it out to sea, he reminded them, there were sharks to contend with—they'd seen plenty of them during their aerial reconnaissance of the island.

Barnes suggested that only the four who were in favour of the idea would try it. If any of them managed to mirror-signal one of the Tactical Reconnaissance aircraft, when picked up by the HDML they'd tell them to proceed close in to Cape Saum the following night and signal with a light flash each hour after 2000 hours. Then the remaining four men could swim out from the beach to the HDML.

As a plan it was agreed it left a lot to be desired. Splitting the team wasn't ideal. The two signallers were still eager to retrieve the radios from the cache and try them, pointing out that if they made contact with the HDML, the boat could come in close to Cape Saum and pick them all up. They disagreed that the Japanese would instantly direction-find the radio, and even if they did, they needed two—preferably three—fixes to get the transmitter's approximate position. If they used the radio carefully, and maybe changed locations after each transmission, the enemy would be kept guessing.

Barnes and Gubbay remained against the idea and seemed even more enthusiastic about the sea attempt. So it was settled: four men would try and four would remain.

At approximately 0330 hours on the morning of Friday 13 April, the four men set out from Cape Barabar paddling behind small logs. On the beach Sergeant Weber, Sapper Dennis and Signallers Hagger and Chandler watched them fade into the night towards the reef, then turned and headed back into the scrub to rest until morning.

Lieutenant Barnes, Lieutenant Gubbay, Corporal Walklate and Private Eagleton were never seen again.

20. SIXTH DIVISION HQ, AITAPE:

13 APRIL, 0700 HOURS

The morning briefing was attended as usual by representatives of most units, but with a notable absence of senior HQ staff. That day the acting Minister for the Army, Senator James Fraser, was scheduled to arrive on a fact-finding and 'morale boosting' visit, so much of the briefing was concerned with his itinerary. The official war diaries of Sixth Division HQ later described the event as follows:

> Senator Fraser visited 2/3 Aust Field Regt, the War Cemetery, 71 Wing RAAF and 2/11 Aust Gen Hosp. At each unit he visited, he talked to many of the troops. At night he broadcast the Prime Minister's message to the troops from the local broadcasting station at Aitape.

However, everyone from the Commander of the Sixth Division down to the humblest private regarded visits by politicians as annoying diversions and many senior staff officers, knowing Senator Fraser was to be at Aitape that day, absented themselves from the HQ area. Fraser had a reputation as being a 'pompous prick', so his visit was carefully orchestrated to float him around Aitape on a schedule that would cause the least disruption.

Consequently, the morning briefing barely touched on operational matters—there'd been little happening during the night anyway. Except for a few items that included a successful ambush in the Torricelli Mountains that killed six Japanese and a report from SRD that their Muschu patrol hadn't kept their first rendezvous, the evening had been a quiet one.

The G3 Intelligence Captain Roland McKay, had hoped to learn that the Muschu operation had been successfully completed and pressed for more information. The Officer Commanding the SRD's Aitape detachment explained that missing the first rendezvous wasn't necessarily cause for alarm and that the Navy would attempt a second rendezvous that evening. Meanwhile, the Air Force would start Tactical Reconnaissance flights over the area to look for light signals and listen for radio messages from the patrol's SCR36 walkie-talkies.

McKay had been involved with enough SRD operations to read between the lines. The SRD commander was a worried man, despite his confident facade. Z Special was like a big family, and when a patrol was in trouble they all instinctively knew it. Unlike the infantry battalions, who could often go to the assistance of their comrades, they were very limited in the help they could provide. All they could do was hope the patrol was resourceful enough to work their way through whatever difficulties they'd struck.

After the briefing, McKay returned to his office. As he'd been responsible for the renewed interest in Muschu, he felt he had a personal stake in Operation Copper. He'd met the team several times in the work-up to the operation, helped conduct their final briefing and couldn't help but be impressed by their cheerful enthusiasm. Now there was a possibility that the patrol had been compromised.

He sat looking at the wall map trying to think whether there were any facts he'd missed—anything he could have done better that would have helped them on this mission.

■ ■ ■

Captain Tomei had spent the night in his command post. There'd been no more reports of enemy commando activity, nor had the commandos returned to their kayaks and tried to leave the island. He still didn't know how many commandos were on Muschu, and a search during the previous afternoon had failed to locate more landing sites. Questioning the accuracy of the original sightings, late that afternoon he called in all squad leaders involved and carefully reconstructed the sequence of events. The most reliable witness was Corporal Buzuki, who being an experienced infantryman, was able to give precise timings and locations. Although he hadn't actually seen the commandos, his observations were an accurate starting point.

The only sighting had been from three young soldiers assigned to the gardens near Cape Saum. At first they'd described their encounter as a pitched battle against superior numbers, but astute questioning by Tomei quickly revealed that this was an exaggeration by frightened soldiers who'd never been in combat. Not a single shot had been fired by either side in that brief contact.

As for the other incidents—Sergeant Hiroto's execution-style death, the two dead in the huts near Cape Warbu, and the four sabotaged machine guns along the eastern defences—closer examination of the timings of these incursions indicated that it was more likely that there was only one group on the island. It was simply the close sequence of reporting that had given the appearance of multiple commando parties. What was in doubt was the size of this group—estimates ranged from eight to twenty. Tomei favoured the lower figure as it coincided with the capacity of the kayaks found near the beach.

What *did* surprise him though was the rapid movement of the group: they'd travelled in a random pattern around the south-east sector on what looked like an expedition bent on execution and sabotage. The only conclusion he could draw was that they were an advance party intent on disrupting the island's defences before a larger force landed. If their aim was reconnaissance, they would not, in his opinion, have sabotaged weapons in such an obvious fashion. Nor would they have executed his men and left them lying around to be quickly discovered.

Tomei sent out orders to all units commanding them to maintain absolute security overnight and for all to report on hourly schedules. He also conferred with Army headquarters in Wewak, advising them of the situation and requesting that their ready-reaction company be made available the following day to help with the search if required, as previously agreed, reminding them that his garrison had been depleted to boost Wewak's defences.

Headquarters replied that it would assess the situation and if by morning the Australians hadn't been found, they'd consider his request for assistance.

While Tomei preferred an immediate despatch of additional forces, he knew that the late hour made it difficult. Because of Australian air activity, the men would have to be moved across the strait at night, which would require considerable preparation.

He spent the night planning the next day's operations and supervising his men. This was the first time they'd been put under any real pressure since they'd arrived on the island, and for some it was the first taste of what most infantrymen on the mainland experienced every day.

The night dragged slowly, with all units reporting in by field telephone on schedule. Surprisingly, there were no real problems during this period of high alert—it was common for soldiers in such situations to call false alarms, fire at shadows or even their comrades. With the spectre of an Australian death squad on the rampage fuelling his men's imaginations,

Tomei was prepared for anything, but to their credit they maintained discipline.

By morning, tired but pleased by the cohesive effect the alert had on his men, Tomei allowed a 50 per cent stand-down. He then issued orders to all staff and sub-unit commanders to coordinate their search across the island using their best men.

This time, they would flush out and kill the Australians.

■ ■ ■

After an uncomfortable night, once again nursing coral cuts and shivering from their futile attempt to get past the reef on their makeshift raft, Hagger, Chandler, Weber and Dennis decided to move further inland. They knew the Japanese, having found their foldboats, would begin a coastal search, so it would be wise to be well clear of the beach area. As the Japanese seemed to have a dislike for the jungle, they felt the best place to lay up during the day would be in the more heavily timbered hills behind Cape Saum. Then, come dusk, they could move to the cape and wait for the HDML's arrival. That evoked some discussion about how the others had fared. All expressed quiet confidence that they'd be able to mirror-flash a reconnaissance aircraft and pass the message on to HDML 1321. However they all knew that four men floating on logs would be extremely difficult to see from the air—even if they were signalling.

As dawn broke, the four men gathered what remained of their equipment, spread out and headed north-east into thick jungle. There they came across several tracks, which they checked for signs of the enemy, but found none. It seemed as if the eastern end of the island was still deserted, or at least only thinly occupied, but they had no way of knowing—the enemy could be waiting in ambush anywhere. They considered themselves lucky that the attempted ambush at the foldboat hide had been clumsily laid. If the Japanese had been deployed in concealed positions, with their machine guns covering the hide area, and used competent ambush discipline, it would have been all over. Instead, the enemy had been out in the open and made no attempt at concealment. On this point, Sixth Division Intelligence had been right: the troops here were mainly second-line. But that was little comfort now.

After an hour they found a suitable lay-up among tall trees and thorny 'wait-a-while' bushes. Clearing an area with their knives, they covered their tracks and prepared to wait until nightfall.

■ ■ ■

Corporal Buzuki returned to his section early that morning, taking with him two men carrying pails of boiled rice and fish. His men would be ravenous, as they hadn't eaten for almost 24 hours. He'd left them late the previous afternoon under the command of Private First Class Asaki, a soldier who claimed to have extensive experience in jungle warfare. Buzuki's orders were clear: set up an ambush position covering the enemy's kayaks, then wait until morning. If the Australians showed during the night, kill them.

As they hurried along the track parallel to the beach, Buzuki suddenly paused. Ahead he heard voices. For a moment he feared it might be the Australian commandos, then he recognised Private Asaki's voice. He left the track and pushed through to the beach, emerging a hundred metres from the kayak hide. Ahead he could clearly see Asaki and the remainder of the squad standing around, making no attempt at concealment. The two machine guns, instead of being hidden and covering the ambush area, were on the beach aimed out to sea.

For a moment he was consumed by rage: so this is how the jungle warfare 'expert' arranges an ambush! Controlling his anger, he strode along the beach, his rifle at the high port. He was 10 metres away before Asaki even realised he was approaching. Turning, Asaki's jaw dropped when he saw Buzuki bearing down on him. Before he could speak, Buzuki drove his rifle butt into his stomach. Asaki dropped on his knees, gasping for breath.

Buzuki turned on the remainder of the squad. They stood motionless, wondering who'd be next. Instead, Buzuki ordered them to form ranks. They shuffled into position, stared out to sea and tried to avoid his eye.

As Buzuki strode along the line, staring clench-jawed into their faces, the two men clattered along the beach with their rice canisters. Breathing hard, they stopped and lowered the four containers. The squad eyed them hungrily.

Buzuki strode over and kicked the containers with his boot, spilling the contents onto the sand. Pointing to Asaki, who by now had risen to his knees holding his stomach, he ordered that he be escorted back to barracks.

Buzuki then turned on the squad, coldly explaining that he'd shoot anyone who disobeyed his orders, and instructed them to set up a concealed ambush covering the enemy's kayak hide.

21. CAPE SAUM:

13 APRIL, 1800 HOURS

As the sun dropped below the horizon, the four Australians broke cover and headed north-east towards Cape Saum. They quickly located one of the tracks they'd used earlier in the day and spread out, moving quietly along with Dennis in the lead. After pausing several times to listen, but hearing nothing except the buzz and croak of night insects, they arrived at Cape Saum at 2000 hours. A quick check of the defences along the clifftop confirmed they still weren't manned. Skirting around the defences, they climbed down to the beach and found a hide among the rocks.

Again it was a moonless night. A gentle breeze kept the insects at bay and they searched expectantly for light signals from the HDML. The sea was a black smudge, broken only by a faint line of white foam a hundred metres out where the waves met the reef. Occasionally the screech of a night gull broke the silence, and all of the men found they were losing concentration and dozing off. Fighting sleep, they forced themselves to stay alert.

Just after midnight, they heard the muffled burble of diesel engines and knew it was HDML 1321 venturing in close. The thought of Lieutenant Palmer and his crew cruising just a few kilometres away with hot coffee on the stove and fresh corned beef sandwiches waiting was frustrating. Someone suggested lighting a fire, but they knew it would draw the Japanese like moths to a flame, so they had to sit and listen as the diesels slowly faded into the night.

Half an hour later a rain shower passed through the area, drenching them. The breeze dropped and the mosquitoes homed in. Without insect repellent, the men had no choice but suffer their whining attacks. By 0100 hours they'd not sighted any signals, nor had the HDML been heard again, so reluctantly they concluded that Lieutenant Barnes and his group had failed to signal the reconnaissance aircraft. They tried to avoid speculation about the fate of the four men, hoping that the current had swept them to the mainland.

After a brief discussion, they decided their best course of action would be to head back to the foldboats and reassess the possibility of killing the soldiers guarding them. If they could, they'd then make a quick dash out to sea and remain there until the HDML returned after dark. If they couldn't escape in the foldboats they'd head for the equipment cache and retrieve the radios, then move to higher ground and get one of the radios working. Once contact was made with either HDML 1321 or base, they could schedule another pick-up.

If they became separated at any time, they agreed to meet at a water-filled bomb crater they'd passed earlier that evening about 400 metres inland. Failing that, they'd make their separate ways to Cape Samein on the south-western end of the island. From there they could try to swim for the mainland and then make for the Australian lines near Dagua.

They considered moving to the foldboat hide immediately, as they'd become familiar enough with the coastal track system and were confident they could reach the cache in less than an hour. However, it was agreed it would be better to move in daylight—they could make a thorough reconnaissance of the area around the foldboats just in case the Japanese also found the equipment cache and set up another ambush.

Silently they left the beach, headed inland and found a lay-up position in heavy bamboo. There they'd rest until dawn.

■ ■ ■

Cruising offshore at the designated pick-up area east of Cape Barabar, the crew of HDML 1321 had no way of knowing that the patrol had moved further north to Cape Saum. For three hours they motored in a racetrack pattern along the coast between Cape Barabar and Cape Warbu, lookouts scanning for signal lights. The night was inky black and balmy, with a slight swell running before an easterly breeze. At one point Lieutenant Palmer ventured close in to Cape Saum in the off-chance the patrol had for some reason moved further north, but knowing the water there was littered with coral he was forced to come no closer than 2 kilometres. After scanning what they could see of the shoreline and sighting nothing, he went about, then resumed patrolling between Cape Barabar and Cape Warbu.

At 0130 hours a rain squall passed through and the breeze dropped, leaving the water oily calm. Lieutenant Palmer ordered the engines be pulled back to idle and the little ship hove to about 3 kilometres off Cape Warbu, rolling easily on the low swell. Again the lookouts saw nothing on shore, the island a vague brooding mass against the stars. For a few minutes Palmer shut down the engines and allowed the ship to drift, ordering absolute silence. Ears straining, they listened in the vague hope that the patrol was nearby and trying to hail them, but the only sounds were the slap of water against the hull and the faint hiss of waves breaking on the reef. In the tiny radio shack the operators had their high-frequency radios tuned to the patrol frequencies, but all that was heard was the hollow rustle of atmospherics and the occasional fading bleep of far-off Morse signals.

At approximately 0200 hours one of the lookouts reported lights approaching from the direction of Cape Boram on the mainland. Simultaneously, all weapons swung round and safeties clicked off. Palmer gave the order to hold fire as the sound of a diesel motor echoed across the water. The lights coalesced into a landing barge, its deck crowded with Japanese soldiers, talking and laughing as if they were out for a harbour cruise. Totally unaware they were being tracked by a 20 mm cannon, two .50 calibre machine guns plus an assortment of rifles and submachine guns, the barge chugged past about 400 metres away. Sorely tempted, Palmer realised that although they'd be able to decimate the soldiers and sink the barge, opening fire would compromise the Copper team pick-up. Reluctantly he allowed it to pass unharmed. As the barge's lights faded towards Muschu Bay on the western end of the island, he ordered the gun crews to stand down.

After waiting another half an hour he ordered the ship to go about. For the next two hours they cruised the southern coast looking for light signals from the missing patrol, then at 0430 hours having sighted nothing, Palmer altered course and HDML 1321 headed away from the island.

■ ■ ■

Captain Tomei watched the barge nudge onto the beach. The ramp slammed down and 60 marines splashed ashore and formed ranks. These were men of the Kaigun Rikusentai, elite Navy troops from the headquarters guard in Wewak. Tomei had used all his persuasion to have them sent here, calling in favours and promising a number of senior officers additional supplies of pork, fish and the potent native brew that had become popular as a sake replacement.

The lieutenant in command strode up the beach to him, saluted then bowed. Tomei responded, then the lieutenant turned to his sergeant and issued quick orders. The marines would be fed, rested until dawn, then briefed and deployed in the hunt for the Australian commandos.

22. MUSCHU ISLAND:

14 APRIL, 0600 HOURS

The four Australians spent a restless night in their lay-up, damp and cold, plagued by mosquitoes and insects. As dawn came they waited fully alert, watching for signs of the Japanese, while the birds around them shrieked their morning chorus. After an hour the sun had climbed above the horizon and the birds had calmed. With no sign of the Japanese, the men relaxed a little and again went over their plan for the day.

It was apparent that Lieutenant Barnes and his group had not made contact with the Tactical Reconnaissance aircraft or the HDML. While they knew the HDML would return to the rendezvous area off the coast for the next four nights, without torches or radios they had no way of contacting it. One alternative was to use the foldboats to get out to sea and signal the boat using Verey pistols. They'd counted about eight Japanese plus two machine guns at the foldboat hide, and with only one Sten and three pistols among them, even with the element of surprise, killing all the Japanese was a tall order. However, they'd reassess that possibility after reaching the hide. The soldiers looked disorganised and poorly disciplined, so maybe there was a chance it could be done.

The next option was to sneak in and recover the radios from the equipment cache. As this was about a hundred metres further inland from the foldboats, there was a chance the Japanese hadn't yet found it. They were confident if they moved carefully they could get in and out without the Japanese seeing them.

The contingency for this plan would be that on contact with the Japanese, Dennis would provide covering fire with the remaining Sten while the others cleared the area. If separated, the rendezvous for the group would be the water-filled bomb crater they'd found off the track behind the Cape Saum defences. If they failed to make the rendezvous, or if they couldn't regroup, then they were to individually make their way to the western end of the island, attempt to swim the strait to the mainland, then head north for the Australian lines.

After cleaning their weapons and an equipment check, they set off, heading west along the track paralleling the beach. Moving silently, again with Dennis in the lead, it took them an hour to reach an area about 200 metres inland from the foldboat cache. Leaving the track they moved into the undergrowth, then slowly crept to where they could see the large palm tree that marked the cache.

For a moment they thought the Japanese had gone, but after waiting a few minutes they saw that the Japanese were still in positions around the foldboats. However, they'd moved their machine guns off the beach and were better spread out and camouflaged. From this it was obvious that someone who knew what they were doing was now in command, and they decided that with only one Sten gun among them they'd have little chance of killing them all. That put an end to plan one.

Further inland, the radio cache still remained unguarded. After waiting an hour and making sure that they'd spotted all the Japanese in the area, they inched towards the cache, pausing frequently to observe and listen. It took them almost two hours to circle around the foldboat ambush, then swing back again to reach the equipment cache. Collecting the radios they moved silently away, treading slowly through the undergrowth, pausing and listening every 20 metres. Finally reaching the track, they headed for the bomb crater rendezvous.

This time their progress was slow. Several times they heard voices in the distance and they broke track to lie silently in the undergrowth until they considered it safe to move on. It was late afternoon by the time they neared the bomb-crater hide. The team's spirits were high, one remarking that in half an hour they'd have the radio working and be set to get out of the place.

In the lead Dennis suddenly propped. On the track ahead, at the corner of a muddy puddle of water, was a boot print, water still draining into the shallow impression. He signalled the others to be quiet, then crept 50 metres further along the track.

Crouching down, he strained to see around a bend. It was then that all hell broke loose. Rounds spattered into the trees around him and zipped close by. Dropping flat, he returned fire with his Sten, aiming where he thought the fire was coming from. The rest of the patrol, hearing the fire, ran up behind him, broke track and headed into the undergrowth. Changing magazines, Dennis opened up again, spraying rounds on a wide front until the weapon emptied. The Japanese also stopped firing and then he heard the others moving again, making their way deeper into the jungle.

The Japanese again opened fire, this time towards the sound of the men crashing through the undergrowth. Dennis changed magazines, then heard the Japanese talking loudly and moving along the track towards him. One suddenly appeared, 5 metres away heading straight at him, but at the same time the three escaping Australians suddenly resumed their flight. Behind him, more Japanese opened fire in their direction. The enemy soldier in front of Dennis went down on one knee and raised his rifle, but before he could take aim Dennis lined him up and put two rounds in his chest. Without a sound the soldier fell face down on his rifle in the mud. Still on his stomach, Dennis saw another Japanese stride over to the dead soldier and kneel. Dennis put three rounds into him and he fell dead across his companion.

Slithering backwards, Dennis moved into thick scrub and waited. The Japanese fired a few more shots, stopped, then he heard them moving away into the undergrowth.

For almost an hour he lay waiting. Then, looking around, he saw through the bushes that he was only 20 metres from the bomb crater rendezvous. By now he was dry with thirst and knowing the crater was filled with rainwater, he slowly crept towards it. Five metres away he saw the rim was covered with fresh boot prints. Then he noticed bubbles rising near the middle. Cautiously he slid down the bank, dipped a finger in the water and tasted. It was bitter and strangely hot. The Japanese had poisoned it.

He scrambled up the rim, then into the undergrowth. Pausing to get his bearings, he remembered that further up, the track branched north towards the empty garden village they'd searched the previous morning. There was a small stream nearby used to irrigate the crops and he could fill his canteen there. Crouched low and staying on the edge of the track, he moved forwards to the perimeter of the gardens. The stream was on the far side of the clearing near a line of trees. He waited a few minutes and, seeing no one, decided to move around the perimeter behind the huts rather than cross through the gardens.

Staying in cover, he made his way around to the line of huts. They seemed deserted. Carefully he moved along the narrow track behind them. Without warning a Japanese soldier, carrying his rifle at the high port, stepped out from behind a hut only a few metres in front of him. Startled, the Japanese soldier panicked and with his rifle still pointed to the sky, pulled the trigger. At the same time Dennis squeezed off two rounds from his Sten, hitting him in the chest. The soldier dropped forward, dead.

Dennis backed up quickly then left the track, cutting into the undergrowth until he reached an area covered by tall grass. Dropping into cover he remained there waiting for signs of pursuit, but none came.

The light was fading now and Dennis was tiring. He decided to backtrack, circle the garden, then make for the rendezvous again to see if the others had returned. If not, he'd set out for the western end of the island. Checking his bearings, he found the track back to the gardens and moved quickly along it. As he approached the spot where he'd shot the last Japanese he heard voices, so he took cover behind a fern tree. To his right he then saw four Japanese stealing along another track that emerged just a few metres away. Unable to move further around behind the fern in time and knowing the Japanese would see him, Dennis levelled his Sten and shot the leader. He then fired a six-round burst into the others and heard a groan and a yelp of pain. Not stopping to see the results, Dennis bolted down the track for 200 metres, then headed north into the jungle until he was satisfied he wasn't being followed. Nearly exhausted, he searched until he found some heavy undergrowth. Unable to go any further, he decided to make this his lay-up for the night. Crawling between the thick roots of a tree, he made himself as comfortable as possible and prepared to wait out the night.

23. SIXTH DIVISION HQ, AITAPE:

14 APRIL, 1600 HOURS

At the afternoon briefing, the SRD detachment commander announced that as the Operation Copper team had failed to make rendezvous with HDML 1321 on the nights of April 12 and 13, it was likely the patrol had run into 'unexpected difficulties'. The Navy would, however, continue patrolling the area: HDML 1321 was due to be relieved on station by a Fairmile—a larger patrol vessel—which would remain in the area, checking the alternative rendezvous points for the next four nights. Tactical Reconnaisance aircraft would also continue their flights twice a day in accordance with the contingency plan, but as yet they'd sighted nothing.

The chances of all the patrol's radios failing simultaneously were remote. They'd either lost them or were being prevented from using them. Coupled with failure to make the rendezvous, the outlook, while not yet hopeless, 'wasn't favourable'.

There was a moment's silence from those gathered at the briefing, as the realisation sank in that the eight men were probably dead or had been captured by the Japanese. However, everyone had become accustomed to the setbacks of war—there'd be time for grieving later.

The briefing resumed, moving on to the next item, a review of Senator James Fraser's visit to the Aitape area. It seemed the Senator's 'meet the troops' soiree had resulted in a welter of complaints to the politician, who'd beaten a hasty retreat to the officer's mess before boarding his C-47 back to Australia. There was a faint ripple of laughter.

After the briefing, Captain McKay spoke in private with the SRD commander, asking if anything more could be done for the Muschu patrol. The commander merely shrugged and reminded him there was still hope. But, he added, seeing that there'd been no radio communication, even what little hope they had was fading. The patrol could be hiding somewhere on the island well away from the coast, but this was a long shot. And even if they were, unless there was some means of flying in and plucking them from the jungle, nothing could be done for them.

■ ■ ■

Captain Tomei was starting to doubt his own judgement. He'd just received reports from the eastern sector telling how three more men had been shot dead and another two wounded. There were no reports of enemy casualties, and conflicting reports about their numbers. It seemed the commandos were everywhere, yet nowhere, setting ambushes or dashing through the jungle taunting his men, then turning and killing them.

Again he realised that in the initial confusion of contact, these reports tended to be exaggerations. So calling in his staff and the lieutenant commanding the marine detachment, he confronted them with the problem and set about coldly analysing the situation.

After half an hour they arrived at the following conclusions.

Enemy forces: it was likely that two groups of eight Australian commandos had landed on the night of 11 April—one group near Cape

Barabar, the other of size unknown in an area yet to be determined, probably near the Cape Saum defences, which were unoccupied at the time.

Enemy intentions: sabotage and reconnaissance.

Course of action: prevent further sabotage of defences; kill or capture the Australian commandos.

Captain Tomei's adjutant reminded him that capturing a prisoner would be most desirable. As the invasion of Wewak was expected soon, HQ 18th Army was most anxious to learn what they could about the Australians' plan and seeing that the commandos were obviously a prelude to the invasion, there was a possibility they would have useful information.

Captain Tomei agreed. Over the next hour they worked out a detailed plan. First they'd man all the defences at the eastern end of the island. Then using the marine detachment, starting at dawn, they'd search the area west of those defences where the commandos were last reported, the aim being to corner them or drive them south towards the sea.

In addition, all other defensive positions around the island would be occupied. However, harvesting and food gathering would continue, with all work parties fully armed and sentries posted.

A comprehensive field telephone reporting procedure would be implemented and additional cable laid to those gardens being worked but not yet linked to the telephone network.

Tomei wanted everything to be in position by morning. The marine lieutenant agreed that his men could move by night. He'd take four squads—40 men—and march them quickly to the eastern sector via the track. It would involve some risk of ambush by the Australians, but he doubted they would be equipped for the type of intentional ambush that could cope with 40 men at night. He also knew Australian tactics—if his men moved well spaced, there would be no way they could be overwhelmed by eight or even sixteen men. Equipped with one light machine gun for every squad, his men would probably overwhelm any attacker who dared set upon them.

The other twenty men could remain here in reserve, ready to move quickly to any point on the island at a moment's notice.

His marines also brought with them two backpack radio sets. This would give them a distinct advantage while deployed, enabling him to split his force into two groups, yet coordinate them and remain in contact with headquarters.

After thoroughly examining the plan, orders were drafted and despatched by runner and field telephone to outlying units. Tomei was confident that by this time tomorrow, he'd be done with the Australians and life could return to normal.

24. MUSCHU ISLAND:

15 APRIL, 0500 HOURS

An hour before dawn, a rain shower passed over the island. Dennis woke and was able to drink from water channelling off leaves and collecting in dips in the ground. The rain stopped before he could fill his canteen, but he knew he'd be able to find more water later. He'd slept fitfully, insects and nervous adrenaline combining to make deep sleep impossible. However, gone was the utter exhaustion that had descended on him at the end of the previous day. Apart from a welter of cuts, bruises and insect bites, he was in good condition. He still had his pack, with emergency rations, medical kit, Sten, spare magazines, knife, maps and compass.

Now all he had to do was avoid contact with the enemy and make his way to the western end of the island.

Then swim five kilometres through shark-infested water.

Then walk 20 kilometres through enemy-held territory.

Then find the Australian lines and hope they didn't see him first and shoot before he could identify himself.

For a moment the enormity of what he was attempting overwhelmed him. But he shrugged it off. The only way to deal with the situation was to take it one step at a time. No point worrying about what might happen, just deal with things as they came. It was a philosophy his family had always lived by and it had served him well.

He thought about his mother, wondered how she was coping. She had no idea that he was stuck on a tropical island swarming with Japanese hell-bent on killing him. Probably just as well, he thought—not for her sake but for the Japs. She was a tough woman who'd raised six children after his father's death and, being born in the bush, could ride, shoot and rope a steer with the best of the drovers. Let her loose here and all the Japs would soon be lined up, caps in hand, having their ears and fingernails inspected for cleanliness.

And then there were his three sisters, always scheming ways to annoy their big brother. He wondered about the youngest, Alice. She was expecting her first child this month. His two brothers would also be oblivious to his predicament. One was in the Air Force, a mechanic who could repair an aero engine with chewing gum and baling wire, the other too young to join up, yet itching for the day he could fulfil his comic-book fantasies about beating off the enemy with nothing more than a cricket bat.

Dennis wondered about the others in the patrol. Where were they? Had they been captured? During the night he thought he'd heard the Japanese taunting him, calling for him to give himself up. Once he swore he heard Mike Hagger shout 'Don't let the little bastards get you . . .' But at night when drifting on the border of sleep, the mind does strange things. He put it down to an overworked imagination fuelled by exhaustion.

His first aim was to make sure he could still fight. As soon as light permitted, and after checking to ensure there were no enemies around, he disassembled his Sten. A perversity of most weapons is their ability to rust, and at this the Sten excelled. This one had been dunked in the ocean, dragged through mud, been rained on yet still had worked perfectly when called for. Opening the tiny cleaning kit he carried, he quickly cleaned, oiled then reassembled the weapon. After checking the action and finding the bolt slid smoothly, he replaced the magazine, cocked the weapon and applied the safety catch.

He unloaded three of the remaining magazines, then cleaned, oiled and refilled them. After swapping over the magazine on the Sten for one of those he'd cleaned, he unloaded the partially used magazine. After cleaning then reloading it, he put it in his left-side magazine pouch so he wouldn't mistake it for a fully loaded magazine. The other two full magazines he placed in the right-side pouches. In all, he counted 105 rounds. He'd used almost half his ammunition in the brief contacts he'd had so far.

Before he packed away his cleaning kit he checked the oil container, a small screw-top brass tube carried by all Australian soldiers. He'd used almost half its contents, which meant he'd have to ration the oil for future cleanings. If he didn't fire the Sten then it would remain clean a little longer, but to ensure it was always in perfect working order it needed regular attention—preferably twice a day in this climate. He'd have to be careful with the remaining oil: it would be ironic if he ended up with a useless weapon just for the want of a few drops of oil. He screwed the top back on hard, then wrapped the tube in the cleaning rag and tucked it securely away in his pack.

Surprisingly he wasn't hungry, so he decided to eat only after he found more water. His food rations were compressed fruit bars and protein concentrates, and without water they'd set in his bowels like concrete. He'd experienced that before and it was something veteran soldiers avoided.

Shrugging on his webbing, Dennis snapped off a few small tree branches and shoved the stems in his clothing to camouflage his outline, then smeared his face and hands with mud. After checking around him and waiting another ten minutes to make sure there were no Japanese in the area, he left the hide. He'd decided not to use the tracks as the enemy would be on full alert after yesterday's activity and would probably set ambushes along the trails and streams. Instead, he'd cut west cross-country following compass bearings until he was well clear of the eastern sector. The Japanese wouldn't expect him to head for their main base areas, so he felt he had a good chance of staying clear of them.

Before heading off, he decided to make one last check of the rendezvous in case the others had managed to return there. It took about ten minutes to reach the bomb crater, and Dennis carefully surveyed the area from cover. There was no sign of the others and, from what he could see, no new boot prints—certainly none with the distinctive Australian sole pattern. Of this he was absolutely sure. So what had happened to them? If they hadn't been killed or captured, they would be proceeding with the agreed plan—heading west for Cape Samein and then on to the mainland. With luck, they'd all meet and be able to make the crossing together.

Leaving the crater he pushed on through the undergrowth, heading west. The jungle was thick and dark, with motes of light shafting through the canopy and dappling the leafy ground. The insects were now out in force, buzzing, zipping, stinging. After about half an hour, the dense foliage gave way to an area several kilometres wide, covered with high kunai grass and scattered palms. He began crossing the kunai, relieved to be out in the open and away from the insects, even though he was more exposed.

He'd gone about a kilometre when he heard movement not far off, followed by a Japanese voice calling. Quickly he hid behind the drooping fronds of a small palm tree, just in time to see two Japanese soldiers come into view. They were about 10 metres apart, using their rifles with bayonets fixed to poke and prod bushes as they advanced. As they moved closer, beyond the second man, Dennis could see more soldiers stretching in extended line a hundred metres or more. Although they made little attempt at remaining quiet, constantly calling to each other, he could see they were well organised and disciplined.

Fortunately he was in a position beyond the last man at the end of the line. The soldier passed by the palm tree, seeming to look straight at him, but still kept going. Dennis waited until their voices faded, then cut away from their line of advance at ninety degrees for a kilometre, before taking a bearing with his compass and resuming his westerly course.

After another hour he arrived near a small rock-strewn hill, about 30 metres high. Climbing it, concealed in high grass, he used his compass to take more bearings and fix his position on the map. He couldn't get a clear view, but he was able to estimate that he was still about 8 kilometres away from his objective. It was now early afternoon and he knew he wouldn't reach Cape Samein by last light.

After a short rest, he went down the hill and came to a small garden. There were no huts, which meant the garden was only tended occasionally, so he relaxed a little. Scouting around the area he found a narrow track heading west; he could see it hadn't been used for some time, so he decided to risk following it. The track wound through the low scrub, and after about fifteen minutes he came to a small pond. Remembering the poisoned water at the rendezvous, he searched for footprints, found none, then gratefully noticed small fish swimming among the reeds. Even so he tasted the water before drinking, then filled his canteen.

Continuing along the track, he passed a small stone mill used by the islanders to grind sago flour. Again there were no footprints or signs indicating recent use. After another kilometre, the track climbed a steep hill, and at the top he paused to rest.

Suddenly, from a distance, he heard shots. Crouching low, he realised they were coming from another hill about half a kilometre west. There were no rounds heading in his direction, so he assumed the Japanese were either hunting game, or perhaps the other members of his patrol. Sadly, there was little he could do to help them.

He now decided not to remain on the trail in case the shooting party came his way, so he broke track and headed due south until he again came to high ground. Using compass and map, here he was able to make a reasonable estimate of his position, gauging he had another 6 kilometres to go before reaching Cape Samein. With luck, and depending on how many Japanese were around, he figured he'd make it by midday the following day.

The hill was covered by tall trees surrounded by thick cover, which made it a good defensive position. With dusk approaching, he chose to remain there for the night. Settling in at the base of a large tree, he cleared an area and shrugged off his pack. It was then he realised just how sore, tired and hungry he was. With plenty of water, he was now prepared to risk the wrath of the emergency rations, so he broke out the compressed fruit bar, sawed off a portion with his knife and, imagining he was back home, enjoyed his Sunday evening meal.

25. SIXTH DIVISION HQ, AITAPE:

15 APRIL, 1600 HOURS

The staff of Sixth Division now faced a dilemma. All evidence indicated that Operation Copper had failed. However, they were none the wiser as to the future role of the island, nor the condition or location of the naval guns. With the Wewak invasion scheduled to begin in less than a month, it was doubtful whether there'd be time to send in another patrol—and even if there was, doing so without knowing the fate of the Copper team was questionable. It had to be assumed that the enemy was now fully alerted and that new patrols would run a high risk of meeting a similar fate.

Division Intelligence had already requested that the Aitape Signal Intelligence detachment look for any changes in Japanese radio traffic that might give an indication of the patrol's fate, but little had yet been discovered. The Aitape Allied Translator and Interpreter Service detachment confirmed that most of the non-ciphered voice traffic from the island was of no immediate value, comprising the usual supply requests, food production reports and other non-essential traffic.

Reports from the Allied Intelligence Bureau decryption and translation services back in Australia advised similar low-value content with encrypted communications intercepted from the island. Also, as of 14 April, there'd been no mention by Wewak of a commando raid in routine reports to 18th Army HQ in Rabaul. However, this didn't necessarily indicate that the Japanese weren't aware of the raid. After all, reporting a raid-in-progress would involve considerable loss of face, and it was likely that they preferred to wait until there was a positive outcome before reporting such an event.

However, one item did raise a flag with Sixth Division analysts: a series of messages from Muschu to Wewak containing weather observations.

While many enemy headquarters had small weather units that observed and reported regularly, this was a new facility for Muschu. Also, their observations included wind strengths of up to an altitude of 10,000 feet. This indicated that their weather station was more than the usual collection of wind gauges and thermometers normally deployed to sub-units. To calculate winds at different altitudes required meteorological balloons, supplies of hydrogen and a theodolite triangulation system to observe the balloon's ascent. All of this required a highly trained support team and specialised equipment. While such information was often used for aviation purposes, it was also the type of data used by gunnery command post teams to compute gunnery settings for long-range firing.

This was yet another indicator that Muschu was preparing to take part in Wewak's defence.

On 15 April, however, the Allied Intelligence Bureau intercept service was able to inform Sixth Division Intelligence that it had received the first clue as to the patrol's fate. The information was somewhat obscure, being extracted from a radio transmission from Wewak to 18th Army HQ in Rabaul, advising that an Australian commando raiding party of 'substantial numbers' had landed on the island during the morning of 12 April. There had been several contacts with the enemy and the situation was now 'contained and being dealt with'.

What this actually meant was anyone's guess. The lack of actual numbers and no mention of Australian casualties was, however, seen as a positive sign. If the Japanese had managed to kill or capture any of the patrol they would have made it quite clear rather than use such obscure language to a higher headquarters. SRD agreed, but the outlook wasn't good. It was obvious that the patrol was in trouble. All that could be done was for the Navy to continue the night time rendezvous as briefed and hope that the patrol could work their way out of their predicament.

After being relieved by another patrol boat, HDML 1321 arrived back at Aitape during the afternoon of 15 April. Its engines had hardly died when a jeep pulled up to the pier and delivered two intelligence officers who went aboard to interview Lieutenant Palmer. While Palmer's information was detailed—particularly the observations of the island and the mainland during the period they were on station—he couldn't give them any more information about the patrol. In fact, he noted, there'd been a total absence of lights showing on Muschu during this period—they'd cruised the south-east coast extensively and not seen a glimmer. To the debriefing team this was a significant observation. It was probable that the island was on 100 per cent alert, totally blacked out—another sign that the patrol had been detected and was still on the loose.

While this information was in some ways encouraging, the absence of any contact by radio or light signals indicated that the patrol had either lost all their radio equipment or were moving too fast to stop and operate it, particularly the ATR4 sets which required an antenna to be strung into the trees. But that didn't explain why they hadn't used the walkie-talkies—all they had to do was pull out the collapsible antennae and they were on the air. The lack of light signals was an indication that the team had moved away from the coast: if they were on the run it was likely they'd head for thick jungle in the centre of the island where it would be impossible to signal from.

All these assumptions were, of course, only educated guesses. The debriefing team thanked Lieutenant Palmer and his crew for a job well done, then drove back to Sixth Division HQ where they passed on the information to the intelligence staff. Together with the SRD detachment commander, they worked until late that evening, compiling all the information they had in an attempt to assess the patrol's situation.

Unfortunately their conclusions remained much the same. The patrol was on the run, probably in thick jungle away from the coast. If they didn't make rendezvous with the patrol boat in the next few days, they would have to assume the men had been killed or captured. Meanwhile, everyone would just have to wait; there was nothing more that could be done.

Unpleasant as the prospect was, operational planning staff now had to consider what to do about Muschu Island. With time running short and another patrol out of the question, the only alternative would be to 'bomb the island into the stone age' as one staff officer put it. The commander was sure that the 1st Army would be persuasive enough to have the munitions made available now that Intelligence had gathered a strong case supporting such action. B-24s would work over the most likely area for the guns first, then medium bombers—Beauforts and Bostons—from Aitape and Lae could seek out and destroy remaining targets of opportunity. The Air Force liaison officer agreed and a request was prepared for submission. The Australian Navy would also assist by using several of its frigates—including HMAS *Swan*, which was already in the area—to bombard suspected defences along the island's coast.

Meanwhile, as there was still a remote chance that the patrol might make it out, there'd be no action against the island for at least another two days. After that it would become a free-fire zone.

26. MUSCHU ISLAND:

16 APRIL, 0500 HOURS

Dennis woke at dawn. It had rained during the night and he was soaked, the branches overhead providing little protection. His first thought was for his weapon. Despite being held close to his body, a quick inspection showed the Sten's internals were specked with rust—not enough to cause a stoppage, but enough to be of concern. So again he went through the ritual of cleaning the weapon, using more of his precious gun oil. When he'd finished, he figured he had enough left for one more cleaning. After that he'd just have to pray the weapon kept working, unless he could find a gun oil substitute. Some soldiers used animal grease to lubricate their weapons, but here, apart from the bird life, there weren't any suitable animals—though he had heard of one soldier who'd shot a duck, roasted it over a fire, caught the fat and used it on his Lee Enfield.

For a moment he thought about it—not so much about the qualities of duck fat for lubrication, but of eating roast duck, preferably one covered in gravy and surrounded by roast potatoes. It was then he realised how hungry he was. The emergency rations were only intended to last a few days and this was his fourth. He unwrapped his compressed fruit bar, sawed off another chunk, then chewed it in disgust. It tasted little like fruit and had the consistency of the modelling clay he used to play with when he was very young. In fact, he decided, it probably *was* modelling clay peddled to the Army by a fast-talking salesman.

He washed it down with water from his canteen, then unwrapped two of the protein tablets and chewed on them. It wasn't much and certainly no substitute for roast duck, but it was all he had. Maybe later he could risk shooting a bush turkey or even a pig—then he'd have all the food and lubricant he could handle.

A sharp crack echoed nearby. Dennis flinched and pressed back hard against the tree.

Where did it come from?

Again another sharp cracking sound, this time followed by the rustle of a falling branch. Behind him, on the opposite side of the tree, it thudded into the earth with an impact that shook the tree. Weakened by age and weighed down by rain, the branch had given way. When he peered around the trunk, he saw it was buried in the ground like a spear. If he'd been sitting there he'd now be skewered like a butterfly pinned to a collector's board.

Quickly he gathered his equipment, slung on his webbing then moved off. He was still in heavy jungle but the undergrowth had thinned, the soft carpet of leaves making for relatively easy going. Setting a course west by the sun streaming through the canopy, he made good progress. After an hour there was no sight of the Japanese, so he rested a few minutes and drank from his canteen. Again he felt hungry but resisted the temptation to eat or even think about food. He could feel he'd lost weight—his webbing had loosened around his waist, so he adjusted the belt until it was snug again. He remembered how his father had once described him when he was only six years old: 'that boy's going to be like a drover's dog . . .'

He hadn't understood the meaning then and wondered what his father would think if he saw him now. At least his ribs would meet with his father's approval.

Realising the combination of fatigue, hunger and tension was distracting him, he forced himself to concentrate. He needed to fix his position, but that was impossible in thick jungle. He estimated he had about 6 kilometres to go before he reached Cape Samein and it was vital he kept south of the Japanese base area around Muschu Bay.

For another hour Dennis continued west, then the jungle thinned to rising, sparsely covered terrain strewn with volcanic rocks. Climbing, he came to the top of a rise, from where he could see the coast about 3 kilometres south. The sun sparkled off the blue water and he knew somewhere over the horizon the HDML would be waiting. It was frustrating to know rescue was so near.

Further on was a track heading towards the sea, so he decided to risk using it. Carefully he checked and found portions of the track covered in muddy boot prints; however, they'd been eroded by rain, indicating they were at least two days old. Making good time, he'd gone a kilometre when he came to a small thatched hut built into high rocks beside the track. Cautiously he approached, his Sten at the ready. Crouching at the door, he listened, then burst in. The hut was empty, two camp beds and a small bamboo-framed table the only furnishings. For a few minutes he rested, then left the hut and continued south along the track which now ran along the top of a cliff.

He'd gone 50 metres when he found a large automatic weapon of about 30 mm calibre mounted on a tripod near the cliff edge covering an arc of fire that included the beach about a kilometre away. The weapon was in good condition, its breach mechanism covered by oiled canvas. Putting his shoulder to it he heaved, moving it only slightly. Again he heaved, and this time managed to shove it forward until one leg of the tripod skidded over the cliff edge. It toppled suddenly, clattering and crashing down the slope, ripping through the undergrowth and slamming into the rocks below, making a sound like a blacksmith beating steel on a giant anvil. Fearing the noise would attract every Japanese soldier on the island, Dennis bolted along the track, then dived into the undergrowth, crouched behind a large fern and listened, heart pounding.

It was a tatic he learned in his childhood. As kids, they'd raid the local greengrocer's store, sneaking around the back where crates of empty soft-drink bottles were stored. In those days each bottle was worth a penny. They'd grab as many as they could, then later sell them back to the unwary Irish proprietor. This novel form of recycling earned them good pocket money, until the owner woke up to the scam. From then on it became a challenge–they'd still swipe the bottles, but instead cash them in at another store across town.

The store owner then mounted guard on his dwindling bottle cache, the juvenile raiding party coming to grief several times at the end of his boot. Dennis discovered during one of these raids that a simple way to evade his pursuer was to duck around a corner of the lane, lie low until the enraged Irishman thundered past, then head off in the opposite direction. Little did he know that he was developing skills that would later prove to be life saving.

Now, as he waited, he controlled his breathing and rested his finger beside the Sten's trigger. Anyone following him would be greeted by a burst of 9 mm which should take their mind off pursuit long enough for him to escape. After five minutes, no one appeared, so he set out again.

Another hour brought him to a junction where a track angled in from the south-east. Along it, not far away, he could hear voices. Not sure whether they were Japanese or islanders, he skirted around the area through the undergrowth, then came to another track about 3 metres wide that led south. Wheel marks indicated that it had once been used by vehicles, but it was now overgrown with grass. Crouching in the bushes beside the track, he was about to cross when a woman appeared. Carrying a woven basket she ambled past him, unaware of his presence, then disappeared around a bend.

Dennis waited until she was gone, then quickly crossed and headed into the undergrowth. For the next three hours he continued west, seeing and hearing more signs of the Japanese as he neared Cape Samein. At one point the track came to a stream, where he filled his canteen then rested. As he was about to cross the stream, he heard someone humming a tune further along the bank. Cautiously, he peered through the bushes to see a Japanese officer in full uniform at the stream, cleaning his teeth. He hummed and scrubbed away, totally oblivious to Dennis who watched, tossing up whether to put a bullet in his chest or sneak around and slit his throat. Deciding that the sound of the shot or the discovery of the body would alert others, he silently crept away into the undergrowth, leaving the Japanese soldier none the wiser as to how close he'd been to joining his ancestors.

He climbed a small hill and from there was able to glimpse the coast, confirming he was on the peninsula that led to Cape Samein. Down the hill, the undergrowth became thicker and it took him another hour to travel only 1 kilometre. Forcing a way through the tangle of vines was becoming increasingly difficult, and he had to pause to rest more frequently. He'd had little sleep and very little food over the past few days and it was becoming harder to think clearly as well as keep up the pace. However, he had no choice but to keep moving so he fought the temptation to find a hide and curl up and sleep. If he was to beat the Japanese he had to outrun and out-think them. He had to keep moving.

After two hours he again came to the wide track, which was now heading due south and looked to have been recently used. To the north he heard a motor, possibly a barge on Muschu Bay—that meant he was close to the

Japanese base area. Along the side of the track, strung between poles were telephone wires, probably linking headquarters with the coastal defences. Resisting the urge to cut them, as the loss of communications would be detected almost immediately and the Japanese would send a team to fix it, he crossed over and headed west into heavily timbered country.

Although the going was easier after another hour, he found he was tiring. He sat near the base of a tree, took a swig of water, then listened. Far off he could still hear the motor faintly chugging, and immediately around him were the calls of birds and the buzz of insects. A breeze ruffled the trees above, creating dancing patterns of sunlight and bringing the musty smell of the jungle.

For a while he wondered about Hagger, Chandler and Weber. Were they somewhere nearby as they made their way towards the cape? And Lieutenant Barnes and his team. Maybe they'd drifted up the coast and were now on the mainland, heading for the Australian lines at Dagua. Would he get back to Aitape, walk into the hut and find them all sitting around playing cards with a place reserved for him at the table? He could imagine Spence Walklate looking up with a grin and asking, 'What took you so long mate?'

Hopefully they were all safe. He'd known them only a few weeks and yet it seemed he'd known them all his life. But he had a nagging fear that he was now alone.

He wanted to rest but knew he had to reach Cape Samein by nightfall. He was also hungry, almost all his emergency rations gone. What was left he'd save for later–he'd need them to provide energy for the long swim. Again he thought about what he had to do. It was almost 4 kilometres across the strait at its narrowest point to the mainland and he was confident he could make the distance, although in his weakened condition he wondered if he was being overly ambitious. But if he could find some food along the coast, maybe fish or coconuts–anything–he could rest a day to regain his strength, then it would only take him a few hours to make the crossing. Maybe.

Struggling to his feet, he moved on. It was now becoming a matter of determination, putting one foot in front of another, ignoring fatigue while trying to concentrate on checking the terrain ahead for any signs of the enemy. He doubted they'd be searching the jungle for him—there was just too much of it. The big risk would be the tracks where he could be ambushed, but he was counting on the enemy not expecting him to be heading into their main base area. Yet one could never be sure with the Japanese: the only thing predictable about them was that they were unpredictable.

For some reason the Japanese he'd so far encountered were reluctant to follow him into the jungle. They were also noisy—most of them had given their positions away by talking as they moved along the tracks. This was unlike the enemy he'd fought around Wau and Mabu in 1942-43, indicating that Sixth Division Intelligence had been right in their assessment of the quality of the garrison here.

After an hour the undergrowth became thick with wait-a-while vines. Pushing his way through them was exhausting but he forced himself on, parting the vines, twisting and weaving through their clinging grasp as they scratched and tore at his skin. For two hours he moved slowly, then cut and bleeding he suddenly stepped from the undergrowth into a clearing on the edge of a village.

From his position near a cluster of huts the village looked deserted. Crouching low, he moved quickly to a position at the edge of a small overgrown garden that gave him cover and a view into the centre of the village. From here he saw the village was larger than expected, cutting across his path for several hundred metres on either side. Not far away was a woman sitting on a log, suckling a child. Playing around her feet was a small monkey that suddenly stopped, pricked its ears and looked his way. For a moment he thought it had seen him, but then it jumped up on the log and latched onto the woman's breast beside the child.

Slowly Dennis made his way around the edge of the village then, coming to another group of huts, paused, senses alerted. He could smell something—something very familiar, but what it was he couldn't be sure. Peering around the corner of a hut, he saw a group of about twenty men and women sitting around a fire with a wild pig roasting on a spit. The islanders chattered away while they busied themselves weaving baskets and mats.

For a moment Dennis stared at the pig, watching the fat ooze from the plump meat and sizzle into the flames. The aroma was now almost overpowering, kicking his salivary glands into overdrive. He wondered if there was a way he could distract their attention, get to the pig and slice off a chunk. But he knew that was impossible, so he suffered in hungry silence.

From a nearby hut someone called out in Japanese, then a soldier appeared at the door. He strode over to the pig, poked at it with a stick, spoke briefly with one of the men then went back to the hut.

Quietly Dennis crept away, bypassed the village and continued west through light undergrowth. After half an hour he came to another village, this one crowded with Japanese soldiers. Some of the Japanese were playing a ball game, while islanders looked on, clapping and cheering. Again he skirted the village, only to find another 200 metres away. Working his way around this one proved difficult: people seemed to be everywhere, and several times playing children came close to where he was hiding. He lay totally still, wondering what to do if one of the kids found him, but fortunately none did. Eventually he was able to move slowly away to an area covered with low grass only a few metres from the beach.

He was about to check the beach when he heard Japanese voices. A group of about ten came from a track further down the beach, then stripped naked and splashed into the water and started playing like children.

Dennis retreated, quickly finding a hiding place among ferns under a big tree about 20 metres away from the beach. From there he watched the frolicking soldiers until just on dusk, when they left the water and disappeared back up the track. Too late now to move on, he decided to remain for the night where he was. In the morning he'd work out how to get off the island, but all he wanted to do now was sleep.

27. SIXTH DIVISION HQ, AITAPE:

16 APRIL, 1600 HOURS

It had been a busy afternoon for the Aitape Radio Intercept Unit. Located in a high-security area near the northern perimeter of Sixth Division's base, the unit was a combined operation between the Australian and US Army Signals Corps, supported by members of the Allied Translation and Interrogation Service. In three large airconditioned huts partly concealed behind sandbagged walls, the section was equipped with radio equipment capable of listening in to most of the Japanese radio traffic in the Wewak and surrounding areas.

At 1500 hours, one of the duty operators scanning the Very High Frequency (VHF) band heard a conversation between two Japanese that he immediately recognised as being of interest. Triggering a wire-recording machine, he noted the time and frequency, then called one of the translating staff to listen in. What had sparked his attention was the frequency of the transmissions. On 47 megacycles FM, it was a band only recently being used by the Japanese, originating (according to US Signals Intelligence) from new backpack transceivers of advanced design. These were still scarce in the New Guinea area and were usually restricted to elite combat units.

The translator slipped into a seat beside the duty operator and pulled on his headset. A second-generation Japanese-American, the translator was fluent in Japanese as well as several Chinese dialects. After listening for a few minutes he nodded to the duty operator, confirming that what they were hearing was indeed of importance. He then indicated that the direction-finding equipment should be used to locate the transmission's source.

What followed was a well-practised procedure. While the transmissions were recorded, other radio receivers were tuned to the same band and the frequencies scanned to determine whether other stations were involved. The direction-finding antennae were also used to locate the signal's origins. This took several minutes, and involved some careful calculation. As the frequency was relatively new, the process had to be performed manually, as the automatic direction-finding equipment had not yet been adapted to the low end of the VHF band.

After five minutes, it was determined that the transmissions were originating from the Wewak area, probably offshore. If so, they were likely to be coming from Muschu Island. The operators immediately realised this to be of significance as they'd been briefed to listen out for any reference to Muschu and for any hint of the fate of Operation Copper.

Once the transmission's origin was established, other radios were tuned to frequencies known to be used by other units on the island, including the headquarters. The Australian signallers knew that if something significant were happening on Muschu, eventually the Japanese would report it to their higher HQ at Wewak.

After fifteen minutes of what sounded like rather confused chatter between the two stations, strict radio discipline was suddenly applied. The Japanese operators resorted to formalised military speech, then changed frequencies. It took five minutes for the Australian signallers to track them down again. This time they continued to use formal jargon, giving little away.

The intercept session lasted until 1630 hours. Then both stations went off the air. Ten minutes later, as anticipated, Muschu's garrison HQ came on the air with an encrypted transmission. The Australian signallers confirmed that Wewak had replied and acknowledged.

An hour after the incident, transcriptions had been made of the recordings and a preliminary analysis prepared, which were then sent by courier to the office of G3 Intelligence.

■ ■ ■

At 1710 hours, Captain Roland McKay was about to finish for the day and hand over to the night duty officer when the courier from the radio intercept unit arrived. Slipping four typed pages from the heavy envelope he'd been delivered, McKay spread them on his desk. He read the summary first—a half-page describing how a Japanese patrol had been escorting several officers along a track near the eastern end of the island when one of the officers, later referred to as 'the Colonel', had been shot from an ambush position. The patrol had then engaged the enemy in what sounded like a very confusing action lasting about ten minutes.

Equipped with a backpack radio, the patrol had called for assistance from another patrol operating in the area, requesting that they act as a cut-off group to prevent the enemy's escape.

The translators could not accurately determine what happened next due to breaks in transmissions between the two patrols, probably caused by manoeuvring in heavy jungle. However, it seemed both units tried to corner the enemy but failed. One patrol commander insisted that they'd only sighted one enemy soldier and suspected they'd wounded him in the encounter, but the other patrol hadn't managed to react in time and cut him off. This provoked some heated accusations between the two patrol leaders over the radio, until someone stepped in and restored order.

McKay flipped through the radio transcript. There wasn't anything more he could glean from the translation of the conversations between the two patrols. However, it did convey a sense of sudden urgency—perhaps even panic—when the Japanese realised that 'the Colonel' had been shot. The Colonel was obviously an important man, and losing an officer of such rank to enemy action wouldn't look good on anyone's record.

McKay assumed that the Colonel had probably been shot by a survivor—or survivors—of the Copper team. For a moment he felt a wave of frustration sweep him: here were more clues that Z Special survivors were still on the island, yet despite having overwhelming sea and airpower and thousands of troops on call, it was impossible to help them beyond what was already being done. That very afternoon, the Services Reconnaissance Department detachment commander had confirmed the Navy would have a patrol boat at the rendezvous that night and for the next two evenings, and that the tactical reconnaissance flights would also continue during the day.

He turned to the last page of the report. There was a note confirming that the radio intercept unit had also recorded encrypted transmissions from the Muschu garrison HQ after the action and that these had been forwarded to the Allied Intelligence Bureau in Australia for priority decryption and translation. It was likely they'd uncover the identity of the colonel killed in the action.

McKay smiled thinly. He had a distinct feeling he already knew who it was.

28. MUSCHU ISLAND:

17 APRIL, 0500 HOURS

Dawn broke fine and clear. Dennis slept most of the night, despite swarms of mosquitoes that came after sundown. With his face bristled by stubble, he'd grown his own defences against the annoying insects, but they'd persisted and found bare skin around his eyes and ears.

He waited until it was light enough to see clearly, then not hearing any noise crept out from his hide and walked cautiously along the beach, staying close to the tree line. During the night he'd worked out what he had to do. To swim the strait with his weapon and pack, he needed something to float them on—a log, a fuel drum, anything that would support the weight. With so many villages nearby, there was even a chance he'd find a dugout canoe to make good his escape.

He scouted along the beach and 50 metres away discovered four barges dragged up above the high-water mark. They'd been badly damaged, probably by aircraft or naval gunfire. Checking each he found the interiors had been stripped, leaving nothing of use. However, stretched between two of the barges he found a large plank. About 3 metres long and half a metre wide, it was almost as big as the surf skis he'd used as a kid. It would have to do—he couldn't risk searching closer to the villages. Hauling the plank into the scrub nearby he erased his tracks with a palm branch, then went back to the hide.

Now he had to decide whether to set out during the day and risk being seen, or wait until night. The tide was falling and already the reef surrounding the island was exposed, but with only a low swell running he was confident he could cross it, even if he had to walk across the narrow stretch of coral. Another hour and the lagoon would be totally cut off from the sea, which would make it difficult but not impossible to get his plank across. However, the water inside the lagoon was mill-pond calm and he'd be easily seen from the shore.

Again he checked his map, working out a rough heading to the mainland. The nearest landing point was Cape Kolang, about 4 kilometres south-west. Staying on course was going to be a problem; he had to avoid coming ashore in the middle of the Japanese defences further east. There the coast was thick with defensive positions, including heavy machine guns and artillery, all manned around the clock.

Tonight there'd be a partial moon, so once he was within a kilometre of the mainland he should be able to make out prominent features such as Cape Pus or Cape Wom. Much would depend on the currents; however, he figured the tide would still be rising, which would take him well north anyway. Although he was anxious to get going, he knew that his best chance would be at night. He decided to rest until evening, then set out after last light.

Decision made, he broke out his emergency rations. He was now down to four malt-concentrate tablets, so he munched on two and washed them down with water. Later he could risk searching around for extra food, maybe even go back to one of the villages and raid a vegetable garden.

Examining his Sten and spare magazines, he gave them a quick clean, deciding to keep the last of his oil until he'd made the crossing. After submersion in salt water it would need a thorough going over, and he'd need all the remaining oil.

A gentle breeze blew in off the sea and rustled the branches around him. A flock of gulls were circling the lagoon, diving and squawking in the calm water. He leaned back against the tree and dozed.

At about 0800 hours an explosion shook him awake. Reaching for his Sten, another blast erupted nearby and water splattered down around him. Then he heard Japanese voices chattering excitedly. Thinking he was done for, he was about to open up with his Sten when he heard children laughing. Peering from behind a branch, he saw islanders in the lagoon collecting fish floating on the surface. Further up the beach there was another explosion, and more children dashed into the water to collect the stunned catch. A large school of fish had been trapped by the outgoing tide and the Japanese were methodically working them up and down the lagoon, while the islanders filled their baskets and carried them away in production line fashion.

This went on all morning, the children laughing and playing amid the explosions, joined by adults who used spears to hunt down small sharks and rays that darted about the lagoon in panic. It was surprising no one was hurt as the soldiers hurled grenades into the leaping silver shoal, but he could see they'd done this many times before as everyone worked as a team. He couldn't help but admire the way the Japanese and the islanders cooperated.

They stopped briefly for lunch, eating bananas and other fruit, then began again. The fish harvesting continued until late afternoon, when everyone suddenly packed up and returned to the village.

Dennis ventured out and checked the area, hoping that a few morsels had been left behind, but there were none—the collection teams had done their work too efficiently. So, resigned to the fact that he would have to find food elsewhere, he went back to the hide to await nightfall.

He dozed lightly until dusk. Then gathering his webbing, he crept out of cover, listened carefully to the night sounds before moving onto the beach. Here he again paused, crouching in the warm sand. Moving quickly along the beach he searched for his plank, but it was gone. He checked again, thinking he was in the wrong place, but after hunting around he found drag marks in the sand where someone had moved it. Walking towards one of the wrecked barges, he saw the plank on the deck, so he climbed up and quietly shoved it over the side, then dragged it into the water. It was waterlogged and floated low, but there was no time to search about for another.

Removing his trousers, he stuffed them with his boots, weapon and ammunition, then bound them to the plank with vines. Pushing the plank out into deep water, he crawled onto it and used his arms to paddle out into the lagoon.

Although there was only a partial moon, it was very bright. As he stroked away from shore, he expected any moment to hear the zip of bullets around him. But none came, and he soon reached the reef. There was only a low swell and he crossed it without trouble, then headed out into deep water. Breathing easier now, he checked his course by the moon, set himself into a steady rhythm and began the long paddle towards the mainland.

29. OFF MUSCHU ISLAND:

17 APRIL, 1900 HOURS

Four kilometres off the southern coast of Muschu, an Australian Navy Fairmile patrol boat cruised slowly, lookouts scanning for light signals from the shore. The Fairmile was larger than an HDML by almost 10 metres and more heavily armed. It was also equipped with ASDIC for sub hunting and radar, which allowed it to search beyond visual range and cover a greater area in a shorter time. Fairmiles had operated in the waters around Muschu and Kairiru Islands before, acting as blockade vessels, detecting Japanese craft crossing at night between the islands or the mainland, then turning their 40 mm Bofors or 20 mm Oerlikon cannons loose. Using these tactics the Fairmiles had accounted for dozens of Japanese vessels including patrol boats, barges and possibly one submarine found north of Kairiru Island.

Tonight though, they'd been briefed not to fire on any target they couldn't identify as there was a chance a Z Special team would be at sea in their foldboats. It wasn't known whether the Fairmile's radar was capable of detecting such small, low-profile objects, so the lookouts had been warned to keep a special eye out for them. The men needed little encouragement: they'd participated in other Z Special operations and although they didn't know the men on this patrol, there was an affinity between them.

After closing in near the shore after dark, the Fairmile kept up a steady pace along the coast between Cape Saum and as far west as Cape Samein. It was a bright night with a quarter moon reflecting off the calm water, so if the patrol was trying to escape the island there was a good chance the lookouts would sight their kayaks. In the tiny radio shack, listening watch was being maintained on the team's emergency frequencies, but again all that could be heard was the hiss and crackle of atmospherics. At about 2230 hours though, the radio operator pressed a hand to his headset, adjusted the gain on his receiver, then sat bolt upright. He'd heard something—the very faint hiss of a carrier wave tapping out . . .

Dah, dit, dit, dah . . .

It was the letter X, the patrol's call sign.

He checked his receiver's frequency setting. It was 5790 kc, the correct channel for the patrol's walkie-talkie. Hand poised over the Morse key, he was about to transmit the response 'Boxer', but paused. Something didn't fit.

The radio operator knew the equipment used by SRD. Their primary high-frequency radio was the ATR4 set, transmitting on a frequency of 4950 kHz. He checked his number two receiver: it was correctly tuned, but all he could hear from it was the faint heterodyne whistle of far-off stations. At this close range the signal from an ATR4 would boom in.

So why were they transmitting Morse using the SCR36 walkie-talkie? The only explanation was their ATR4s had been lost and the SCR36 was all they had left. Maybe it too was damaged and they were attempting to make contact by keying the press-to-talk switch.

He tapped out the reply on his Morse key. Then waited. There was no reply, so he transmitted again. Nothing.

Calling to his offsider, he briefed him to take over the radio watch. He then went up to the bridge to report the incident to the captain.

The commander listened carefully. Both agreed there was a possibility that the transmission from the island was a ruse. If the patrol had been captured before they'd had time to destroy their codebooks, the Japanese might be trying to confirm the presence of a pick-up vessel in the area by transmitting the call sign in Morse using the walkie-talkie, as an Australian voice would be difficult for them to imitate. Although the brief acknowledgment wouldn't be sufficient for the Japanese to get a fix on them, the commander ordered an immediate change in course, going about ninety degrees and throttling up a few knots to throw the Japanese off their calculations. He didn't want to be the first Australian ship to discover that the guns of Muschu were active.

The operator admitted that it was also possible that what he'd heard had originated a long way away—high-frequency transmissions had the ability to skip off the ionosphere for thousands of kilometres. It was probably just a bizarre coincidence that someone had transmitted the patrol's call sign, or maybe it was part of a longer transmission that had faded in then out again. There were a dozen explanations.

The commander agreed, then ordered the radio operator to continue his listening watch, but not to acknowledge any more transmissions until they'd conferred again.

After another ten minutes, there were no incoming rounds from the island, so the commander ordered the original course be resumed.

30. OFF MUSCHU ISLAND:

17 APRIL, 1900 HOURS

Dennis was two hours into the crossing when the first shark came. He was paddling through calm water alive with phosphorescence, every stroke leaving a fiery trail that flamed and sparkled with blue-green light. He heard splashing behind him, then the hiss off a fin cutting through the water. The shark swept past his right side, trailing phosphorescence, then arced around and headed back towards him. Dennis stopped paddling, raised his arms out of the water and tried to keep his balance as the shark streaked past his left side like a glowing torpedo. It then slowly circled.

For what seemed an eternity the shark cruised around, approaching close, then suddenly turning about as if taunting him. Finally it lost interest and swam lazily away.

It was almost half an hour before Dennis summoned enough courage to resume paddling. Imagination now fired, every stroke in the water left a vivid trail he was sure would attract more sharks. Raised near the ocean, Dennis had talked with fishermen and sailors who all claimed to know someone who'd lost a limb to a shark, and all agreed it wasn't the biting-off that hurt, because sharks had rows of razor-sharp teeth that sliced painlessly–it was only when one had time to gape at the severed appendage that the pain set in. So as he paddled he found he was checking each arm, fearing he'd suddenly find a bloody stump where his hand had been.

Dennis could see down into the black water, where deep below, fish–or sharks–were leaving trails like meteors in the sky. In some way's this was even more frightening than coming face to face with a shark. As a boy he'd read Jules Verne, and who knew what monsters lurked down there? Expecting to be seized by giant tentacles or hit by a shark at any moment he paddled on, trying to remain calm, telling himself that his imagination was his worst enemy. At least with the Japanese he could fight back, but against unknown sea creatures or sharks there was little defence.

After another hour, a rain squall hit, lashing the water, driving waves that broke over him and threatened to wash him off his plank. He clung on, tried to stay head-on to the waves, and waited for the wind to stop. Eventually it did and an eerie calm descended, the water becoming oily and flat. Dennis resumed paddling, judging direction by the moon and straining to see the mainland. However, he'd lost all sense of time and had no idea where he was.

Still the shapes swam past him, below him, around him. It took every ounce of strength to keep going, making one stroke after another . . .

Forget the sharks, if the Japs find you out here at daybreak they'll torture you, then have you stuffed and mounted. You'll spend eternity as a trophy above the Emperor's fireplace . . .

Another squall hit, this one seeming to come from all directions. The rain lashed until it stung his skin and the world around him became choked with foam. Barely able to breathe, he closed his eyes, clung to the plank and prayed he'd survive.

31. SYDNEY:

17 APRIL, 2400 HOURS

In a large brick bungalow in the suburb of Kensington, a light snapped on in one of the bedrooms. Throwing back the covers, Emma Golding found her slippers, then after pulling on her dressing-gown left her room and headed down the corridor. Coming to a door, she rapped on the polished wood, pushed it open and flicked on the light.

In her bed her twin sister Mary opened her eyes and turned to her. Emma quietly told her to get dressed as they had to go to the church.

'Mick needs our help,' was all she said.

Such was the relationship between the two sisters that Mary didn't question her but merely nodded, then went to her closet. It was a cold autumn night and being of slim build she needed to dress warmly.

Ten minutes later the sisters were striding purposefully up the road leading to Our Lady of the Rosary Catholic Church. A heavy fog hung over the city, damp shadows relieved only by the dim glow from the wartime street lamps. Neither of them were afraid of being out at such an hour, for they firmly believed that a higher power watched over them. Tonight they were going to seek the assistance of that deity to protect a loved one.

Emma and Mary were related to Mick Dennis by marriage. Their brother George had met Mick's sister Clare at the 1932 Los Angeles Olympics when she was the pin-up girl of the Australian team. George, then the Australian 200 metres track champion, vowed he'd one day marry Clare, but as she was only sixteen he had to wait until 1937 before he could do the 'respectable thing'. Once married, Clare moved into the big house in Kensington, where she lived with George along with his brother, Emma and Mary.

George was then a detective in the Sydney Criminal Investigation Branch and because he was always pursuing what he called the 'villains of society', he was something of a rough diamond. Being exposed to the underworld, his pragmatic view of life differed greatly from his sisters, and while he hadn't totally rejected the Catholic faith, he regarded religion with a somewhat jaundiced eye. The sisters, though, embraced their religion and became ardently devoted to church work, at one time even considering entering a holy order.

The two families got on well together. Before the war, both families would often gather for Sunday lunch, the women preparing the meal while the men sat around on the veranda drinking beer and discussing Saturday's horse races, the cricket, boxing and politics.

After a huge Sunday lunch, everyone would retire to the drawing room. Here the men played poker and drank more beer while the women talked and indulged in a glass or two of sherry. During those afternoons it was customary for the women to gather around the piano—Emma was an accomplished pianist, and both sisters were beautiful singers, their voices trained from youth in the church choir.

After an hour of vigorous singing, with the men often joining in, the dark side of George Augustus Golding would suddenly emerge. Raised in the outback, he had an incredible memory and had amassed an enormous repertoire of bush poetry. George not only knew every Australian poem ever written, but many that weren't yet on paper. So he'd rise, take the floor and give renditions of 'Clancy of the Overflow' or 'The Man from Snowy River', then sing one or two bush ballads—often launching into the seamier versions of popular Australian verse.

The sisters, despite their prudish facades, would soon be doubled with laughter, but drew the line when he inevitably came to reciting his all-time favourite, 'The Bastard from the Bush'—a bawdy version of Henry Lawson's 'Captain of the Push'.

On hearing this Emma and Mary would excuse themselves, leave the room and prepare for evening mass. On their way out they'd remind George that as he hadn't been to confession for twenty years he should consider making amends with the Lord before it was too late. His reaction was usually predictable—he'd recite another verse, which would send the sisters scuttling out the door, convinced their brother and anyone associated with him was doomed to suffer eternal damnation.

Of particular concern to them was young Mick Dennis, who'd fallen under George Augustus's wicked influence, for he'd taken up a job teaching policemen the ways of cracking skulls and twisting limbs using Oriental techniques that were outside the Marquis of Queensberry Rules. The sisters included Mick in their prayers, along with their beloved but very misguided brother. When war came and Mick was sent to New Guinea with the 2/5th commandos in 1942, they continued their intercession. Despite incredible odds, Mick returned a year later, thinner but whole—living testimony to the power of prayer.

Inspired, the sisters made it their duty to pray for those in the neighbourhood who'd gone to war, irrespective of their religion.

When Mick was again shipped off to New Guinea in late March 1945—this time with a unit whose function they didn't understand, nor could he explain—they resumed their prayers for him, never doubting that he'd return.

So on the night Mick Dennis was crossing Muschu Strait, his sisters-in-law were in the local church praying for his survival. They of course had no idea where he was or what he was doing: all they knew was that he was somewhere in New Guinea and that he was in great danger.

A little after sunrise, Emma and Mary returned to the house and found George eating breakfast before going on duty. Seeing the rosaries in their hands, he didn't press for an explanation. He'd become used to their expeditions to Our Lady of the Rosary Catholic Church; however, this was the first time they'd ventured out on a midnight pilgrimage, so someone must have really been in deep strife—or so they believed.

Emma, noticing the question in his eyes, smiled at him and said confidently 'Mick will be safe now.'

32. OFF MUSCHU ISLAND:

18 APRIL, 0500 HOURS

Dennis had lost track of time. He'd been paddling for what seemed an eternity, his arms feeling as if they'd been pulled from his body, yet they continued in an endless rhythm, pushing him slowly towards the mainland.

Lift, reach, stroke. Lift, reach, stroke.

Dennis had gone beyond fatigue, drawing on strength and a determination he never knew he possessed. Gone too was the fear of the unknown—long ago he'd figured that if the sharks hadn't taken him it was because they'd decided he wasn't worth eating.

So he persisted, setting himself a goal of ten strokes, then another set of ten, then another, not daring to think how many more sets of ten were needed to reach shore, or how many he'd done. He remembered how his sister Clare, a skinny kid who thought she could beat the world, had trained herself for the Olympics. No coach, just the family to encourage her as she stroked up and down the pool in all weathers. She'd be up early, walk alone to the pool in the rain shivering, while he remained warm in bed wondering what was driving her.

She'd endured the taunts, the sceptics in the press who called her the 'fish from Coogee aquarium'—even the jibes from school friends who shunned her because it wasn't considered a girl's place to compete.

Yet she ignored them all and two years later went on to become the world's best. If she could persist and win, so could he.

Lift, reach, stroke . . .

He'd survived three storms, each one more intense, yet somehow he'd remained glued to his plank. He now realised that being waterlogged, it acted like a ship's keel, steadying him against the waves.

Lift, reach, stroke . . .

To divert his mind from his aching arms and the cold that was seeping into his bones despite the tropical water, he thought of home, the family, of those wonderful Sunday lunches in winter, with mountains of roast beef, roast lamb, baked potatoes, peas, pumpkin and steaming boatloads of gravy. And beer—endless brown bottles that marched clinking around the table, crowded the centre and overflowed onto the floor. His brother-in-law George seemed to have an endless supply of beer. But then he had secret hoards of everything. Even poetry . . .

Pity the Japs didn't understand English, he mused. If they did, they could ship George up here and he could quote his own brand of poetry at them until they surrendered . . .

Several times he thought he heard engines nearby, muted and rumbling, but afraid he was imagining them, Dennis refused to stop paddling, fearing that if he did he'd never start again. Then he'd slip off his plank and sink into the deep where strange glowing creatures waited to pick his bones clean. So he went on.

Another ten, another ten . . .

He wondered about Lieutenant Barnes and his group. Were they paddling about on their logs nearby? Where were Chandler, Hagger and Weber? Were they following, or ahead of him? Or had those voices he'd imagined been real? Had the Japs caught them?

Time became meaningless, punctuated by endless stroking.

Below him the water was losing its black mystery as the rising sun shimmered into the depths. It happened so gradually that his numbed mind barely registered the change. A sandy bottom alive with fish gradually came into focus. The sun sparkled across coral. A crab scuttled along the bottom and burrowed into the sand. Swarms of fish darted. There was a world down there going about its business, oblivious to his presence. He stroked on, watching the fish, seeing nothing there that could harm him and wondering if he'd really been afraid. The sand came closer, rippled like dunes in a desert. It looked so close he could reach out and touch it. His hands were now stirring up clouds with each stroke.

Something bumped against the plank. Annoyed that a shark would dare attack him now, he looked up to see the plank was nudged up against a beach. Twenty metres beyond was jungle tinged by the rising sun. He blinked, then looked back over his left shoulder. The sun had only half risen above the water and low on the horizon he could see Muschu Island.

He was on the mainland. But where?

Then he froze. Among the palms ahead was a large concrete bunker, and in it, a gun with a barrel the diameter of a sewer pipe aimed directly at him. For a long moment he stared into the muzzle, expecting his world to end in a sudden flash. The irony was overwhelming: he'd come so far, and by a fluke of rotten luck ended up at the wrong end of a Japanese artillery piece.

He waited.

Nothing happened—no flash, no shots, no shouts or swarming Japanese. Rolling off the plank, he untied his gear, then finding his legs were numb, collapsed in the shallow water. Forcing his body into action, he dragged himself up the beach and lay beneath the weapon's barrel. Suddenly it didn't look so threatening. Just a lump of iron painted dull green.

After massaging his legs he was able to stand. Clutching at the concrete walls, he gingerly hobbled into the gun emplacement for a quick look around. The gun was an 80 mm weapon—a quick loader capable of punching out about ten rounds a minute, accurate against aircraft or shipping. It was clean and well maintained, with ammunition canisters stacked ready around the walls. From the look of the place it was regularly manned. Deciding sabotage would not be a good idea, he checked outside and found a small cooking area built into the wall with a kerosene stove. There was no food.

Removing his gear and boots from his trousers he dressed quickly in the soggy clothes. Checking his Sten, he dragged back the bolt and applied the safety. It was rusting, but though a little stiff it moved smoothly. He'd clean it later. There was no time now—he had to get clear of the area.

Twenty metres behind the emplacement was a dirt road running parallel to the beach. From the tyre marks and footprints it was obvious the road was used regularly, at least up to the gun emplacement where the tyre marks made a wide circle. Further north, it was overgrown with grass. He crossed the road and found a hiding place among tall bushes. There he took his map from its waterproof wrapping and laid it flat. After sighting along the coast and across the strait, he calculated he was at Cape Pus on the northern fringe of the Wewak coastal defence zone, well south of his intended landing point. That meant it was about 30 kilometres to the Australian lines near Dagua—maybe less if he could find one of the Australian patrols from there that were pushing south towards Wewak.

The easiest route would be to remain close to the coast, where there were plenty of roads and tracks—but also plenty of Japs. If he went inland, he had a better chance of avoiding the enemy, but inland the terrain deteriorated into steep hills and plunging valleys clogged with jungle. To make any progress he'd have to stay on the tracks, and that meant risking being seen by the Japanese. So he had no option other than staying with the tracks while hoping he could remain alert enough to see the enemy before they saw him.

He decided to try the coastal route first. The dirt road he was now on looked as if it was once well used, so it probably linked their coastal defence positions as far north as the Hawain River. Chances were the Japanese weren't patrolling the road, as they would be expecting the Australian advance to come from the north.

Folding his map away, Dennis was about to settle in and clean his Sten when he heard a vehicle approaching from down the track. Peering between branches, he watched as a truck pulled up at the gun emplacement and eight Japanese soldiers climbed out. They chatted as they unloaded a Juki machine gun and two boxes of ammunition, then fixed the gun on a tripod beside the emplacement. After loading a tray of ammunition, they sat down and began lighting cigarettes and talking. The truck driver joined them, carrying a small bag of rice as one of the crew lit the kerosene stove and prepared to boil water in a large pail.

It was obvious this was their daily routine: cook up tea and rice, then spend the day hoping no one attacked while lazing about in the sun. Dennis smiled. Not a bad life actually—pity for them it would soon be spoiled by the Sixth Division. He watched one of the soldiers pull a throw net from his pack and hang it out to check the weave. There were plenty of fish about, so they'd probably net the high tide and cook the catch for lunch.

Dennis groaned. He was down to only two malt tablets and even the sight of boiling water was making his stomach rumble. For a moment he toyed with the idea of taking their food. They were all bunched together, and being only 20 metres away would make an easy target. But common sense prevailed. Even if he did manage to get them all, the firing would alert others to his presence.

Then Dennis realised he might have to kill them anyway. If the Japanese looked at the beach they'd see the plank and the marks in the sand where he'd dragged himself ashore. Even from his position almost 50 metres away, he could see it laying there like a giant finger, pointing accusingly.

He watched the soldiers closely, holding the Sten and wondering if it would fire reliably without its daily cleaning. It had just spent more than eight hours totally submerged in salt water so it was anyone's guess.

One of the Japanese strode to the front of the gun emplacement, where he stood looking out over the water while urinating onto the beach. Dennis held his breath: the soldier could surely see the plank and the footprints, but fortunately he was more engrossed in making piss patterns in the sand. For what seemed an eternity the soldier pissed away, with Dennis wishing he had a Welrod. One slug in the right place and the soldier would be spouting like the Archibald Fountain.

Eventually the performance ended and the soldier went back to his mates and sat down. Fortunately they were all now too engrossed with preparing breakfast to bother with anything else. If they sat around long enough, the rising tide would erase the footprints and the plank would be just another piece of driftwood. Dennis could see the water lapping in now, moving quickly over the sand. Another ten minutes and all trace of his arrival would be gone.

The Japanese were now looking at photos, their lewd gestures a clear indication of what sort of photos they were. Someone lit a cigarette and passed around the pack. Dennis noticed the smoke was drifting north.

He decided the best move would be to put as much distance between them as possible. Gathering his webbing, he crept from the hide, then cut quietly further into the scrub until he was out of sight, then made his way north parallel to the road for half a kilometre before cutting back to it again. Here the road was overgrown with tall grass, with no footprints or signs of other traffic. Walking close to the side of the road he pushed on north.

After fifteen minutes he paused. The sun was above the trees and he estimated the time was about 0700 hours. Already the air was warm, tempered slightly by the sea breeze. Leaving the track, he moved into the undergrowth about 20 metres and found a lay-up near a large tree. Here he could regroup, clean his weapon and get ready for the long trek north to Dagua.

33. ALLIED INTELLIGENCE BUREAU, BRISBANE:

18 APRIL, 0730 HOURS

The day watch had just taken over duty when a decrypted message was brought to the attention of the section head. It was a situation report from the Japanese 18th Army in Wewak to Rabaul HQ, summarising events over the past 24 hours. Among the items was a reference that was immediately flagged as being associated with Operation Copper.

'17 April, 0600 hours: Two enemy commandos killed on Muschu.'

The analyst who'd found the reference had been briefed to look for any mention of the lost patrol. This was the second she'd found since they'd landed on the night of the 11th. The brevity of the entry was puzzling, as there'd been no further mention of the size of the patrol, or the fate of the remaining men.

The section head instructed the analyst to re-examine 18th Army traffic over the past three days to see if there was anything they might have missed. Meanwhile, a signal was drafted and sent to 1st Army HQ in Lae. From there the information was passed down the command chain on a limited, need-to-know basis. Recipients included Sixth Division HQ at Aitape and the SRD detachment commander at Lae, Major Richard Cardew.

On receipt of this information at around 0800 hours, Cardew immediately organised a flight to Aitape. Knowing that only two of the patrol had been reported killed raised a glimmer of hope: six were still unaccounted for. If the Japanese had captured or killed them, they would've been boasting about it to Rabaul. Chances were they were still alive. So where were they? There'd been no sightings, no radio messages, not a scrap of evidence to indicate their fate.

While Cardew knew that all that could be done was being done, like any responsible commander he needed to make sure for himself. He knew the Navy had put several patrol boats at the Sixth Division's disposal, so he signalled his detachment commander at Aitape, requesting him to arrange for one of the boats to be made available. Within twenty minutes a message came back that HDML 1321 would be fuelled and ready to go early that afternoon.

At 1100 hours Cardew landed at Tadji airfield where a jeep was waiting to take him to Division HQ. There he conferred with HQ staff, including the G2 Operations, G3 Intelligence and the Officer Commanding the Aitape SRD detachment. Considering the latest information and the possibility that survivors of the patrol were in hiding somewhere on Muschu, it was agreed to postpone any action against the island, pending further advice. The information had arrived just in time, as the first B-24 raid was scheduled for the following morning. Thirty-six aircraft were going to bomb the south-east coast area where the guns were suspected to be, followed by more attacks along the coast during the day by Beauforts from Tadji.

During the flight to Aitape, Cardew had also put together a plan to locate and rescue any survivors. It was a gamble, and one he knew should be put 'through channels' for consideration. But there was no time for such luxuries. When he outlined it at the staff meeting, the G2 Operations agreed it should go 'upstairs' for a decision. But as the SRD operated almost autonomously, it was felt that if Cardew could pull it all together in the little time available, he should be given every support. They would deal with the paperwork later.

One problem would be the Air Force: Cardew's plan needed their cooperation. In the closing phases of the Pacific War, the RAAF had become increasingly bureaucratic. The Chief of Air Staff had introduced strict new rules concerning the employment of aircraft in support of Army operations, even going as far as requiring approvals sought from Operational Command Headquarters in Australia for missions in New Guinea that had previously been almost routine. Fortunately, most tactical commanders realised the stupidity of this and where possible ignored the decree.

The G2 sent for the RAAF Liaison Officer, Warwick Masters, a squadron leader who'd been in New Guinea since the early days and who'd flown in the Battle of Milne Bay, a turning point in the New Guinea campaign. It was there the Australian Air Force performed a miracle of ground support, their P-40 Kittyhawks barely getting airborne from the jungle strip before opening fire on the attacking Japanese. They'd burned out gun barrels in that battle, coming in to rearm, then taking off to continue the fight when the enemy was firing on the airstrip. The squadron leader was a man who knew the realities of warfare and had little time for the desk-bound Chief of Air Staff.

When Cardew explained his plan, the squadron leader raised his eyebrows, smiled, then replied: 'No worries, Major.'

When reminded that an operation of this nature could place a pilot in extreme danger, he merely shrugged, adding: 'Easy way round that. I'll fly the sortie myself.'

At 1230 hours Cardew was driven down to the harbour, where he went aboard HDML 1321 and spoke with the commander, Lieutenant Palmer. Cardew had a proposition for him. He wanted to know if it was possible for the boat to get closer to the island—close enough for any survivors to swim out to the HDML. Cardew knew it was asking a great deal, as the coast was littered with uncharted reefs and it would put the ship right under enemy noses.

Palmer understood. He gathered the crew together and explained the situation. For a brief moment there was silence, then someone firmly replied: 'Anything for the Z blokes, skipper.'

Half an hour later, with Cardew on board, HDML 1321 slipped its moorings, headed out of the harbour past the gathering invasion fleet, and set course for Muschu Island.

34. PNG MAINLAND:

18 APRIL, 1100 HOURS

After travelling along the fringe of the road for several kilometres, Dennis came across six trucks parked on the beach side of the road. The trucks were covered over; most of them were disused. At the same time, he spotted a reconnaissance plane off the coast, flying low over the water. Dennis jumped out of cover onto the beach and waved frantically at the plane—to no avail. The pilot didn't see him.

Dennis watched the aircraft disappear north. In twenty minutes it would be landing at Tadji. It seemed almost unjust. Here he was, half starved, staggering through enemy territory while an Air Force ace zipped by in shirt sleeves at two hundred miles an hour on his way back to civilisation. The pilot would soon be enjoying a shower, clean clothes and good food. Plenty of food.

He laughed. Who's the mug then?

Heading back into the undergrowth, Dennis crouched low and listened. It had been risky exposing himself in that way and he'd think twice before doing it again. Hearing nothing, he relaxed a little. The sun was now high and he was sweating heavily, so he took a long drink from his water bottle, then wet his hair and face. He'd need to find water soon, but that shouldn't be a problem: last night's rain had filled many of the creeks and bomb craters.

Again he checked his Sten. He'd used the last of his oil to clean it after the long swim and he'd spread it thinly. Removing the magazine he examined the base of the first round, looking for signs of corrosion, but there were none. Although he'd cleaned all the magazines, he was wary of ammunition that had been in sea water for over eight hours. Fortunately everything looked in good condition, so he eased the bolt forward and replaced the magazine.

After looking at his map and calculating his position, Dennis moved back to the edge of the road and continued north. After another kilometre, the road suddenly ended. A rusted bulldozer peppered with jagged holes lay on its side like a discarded toy; for a hundred metres around, the trees were shattered stumps among water-filled bomb craters. Many of the craters were already sprouting lush grass around the rims, the result of the explosive's fertilising effect.

Skirting around the area, he moved into the undergrowth and continued walking, staying about 50 metres from the beach. After ten minutes, he paused. Ahead he could hear Japanese voices calling out and the sound of someone chopping wood. Probably a Japanese camp where they were building defences or gathering timber. For a while he listened, trying to gauge its size, then decided the safest course would be to move further inland and bypass it.

Heading due west through light scrub, he found a little-used track that climbed into hilly country. Reluctantly he stayed with it, avoiding other tracks crossing it that were covered with fresh boot prints. After about an hour the track levelled and wound through thin scrub along the top of a narrow ridge, with steep drops on either side. The track was slippery from rain and Dennis cautiously picked his way along the muddy trail.

Coming around a bend, he froze. Ahead were two Japanese soldiers walking towards him, one behind the other. He stepped to the side, pressed into the bushes and cocked his Sten. Suddenly they saw him and panicked. The first soldier tried to swing his rifle up to fire, but in doing so slammed the butt into his mate's stomach. Knocked sideways the soldier yelped, slipped off the track and rolled screaming down into the ravine.

At the same time Dennis aimed and squeezed the trigger. The bolt slammed home with a hollow clunk. Misfire.

Hands working instinctively, he tried to clear the weapon while charging directly at the Japanese soldier, knowing his only chance if the Sten failed again would be to get under the man's guard and beat him to death. Instead of taking an aimed shot, the soldier shrieked, turned and fled. Before Dennis could fire again he had vanished.

Heart pounding, Dennis ran along the track until he was clear of the ridge, then scrambled into the bushes and lay low. Checking the Sten, he found a twig lodged in the side breach mechanism, preventing the bolt from closing and the firing pin from striking the round. A small problem, but enough to kill the user—a snag the Australian Owen gun, with its down-facing ejector port, rarely encountered.

Aware that the Japanese soldier would be heading back to raise the alarm, he knew he had to put as much distance behind him as possible. For a moment he allowed himself to speculate about how the hapless soldier would explain the incident. He could hardly admit that he'd clumsily butt-stroked his mate over a cliff, then when faced by a single Australian he'd done a bolter. That sort of confession would earn him an invitation to commit *seppuku*—if he was lucky.

Ironically, to save face, the soldier would probably claim the ridge was swarming with Australians, and the result would be a hoard of sword-waving Japs heading his way at any moment. Regretting he hadn't cleared the Sten quicker and put a few bullets between the retreating soldier's shoulder blades, he set off at a brisk jog. For half a kilometre he remained on the track as it descended, expecting at any moment to be confronted by the enemy. After reaching a junction of three tracks, he decided to remain clear of all trails for a while, so after pausing to listen, he struck out across low scrub for ten minutes, then turned back onto a northerly course.

For an hour he made good progress, but then came to a sago swamp that ran east-west across his path. Wading through it was out of the question: the swamps and rivers on the coast swarmed with crocodiles, and although he'd overcome his fear of sharks, Dennis wasn't inclined to test his courage against reptiles that had developed a taste for human flesh. The only way around it was to head east. He followed a track around its edge, then managed to cross over near the coast, but further on ran into a succession of small Japanese encampments spread over a wide area. Picking his way around them took almost two hours. Then, after narrowly avoiding a group of six Japanese soldiers who suddenly appeared as he was crossing a dry creek, he decided the coast was too dangerous, so he headed inland again.

He was now tiring badly. Finding a clump of bushes, Dennis paused to rest. This was the sixth day of the mission and he knew the strain, lack of sleep and want of food was affecting his judgement. He estimated he'd travelled less than 5 kilometres north since landing at Cape Pus, but with all the diversions to avoid the Japanese he must have travelled twice as far. At this pace it would take him a week to reach Dagua. Without food he knew he'd never make the distance. He'd stretched his emergency rations further than they'd been intended and although it was possible to live for many days without food, he also knew it wasn't possible to spend most of that time climbing up and down mountains being pursued by the Imperial Japanese Army.

So there had to be a way. Food was a priority. Maybe a local village was the answer—there were plenty of them around. Find one, locate their garden and dig up the crop. But even that wasn't so straightforward. Many of the yams and other vegetables the Papuans grew needed to be specially prepared and cooked—eat them raw and a grown man could be reduced to a mindless husk in minutes.

The problem wasn't so much in finding food. He'd learned to live off the jungle during his time with Kanga Force, even though in some areas such as the highlands there wasn't much food to find—the New Guinea jungle wasn't the fertile Garden of Eden some people imagined. The real problem was that he needed a base from which to forage or hunt. In the heart of Japanese territory this was almost impossible—anywhere else it would have been easy, especially along the coast.

And then there was the simple matter of all the information he carried. He now had detailed drawings of most of the major defensive positions on Muschu Island, and this information had to be delivered. His priority was to get it back to Sixth Division—he owed it to his mates.

So after a short rest he pushed on. One step at a time.

35. TADJI AIRFIELD:

18 APRIL, 1530 HOURS

Squadron Leader Warwick Masters clambered onto the wing of the Boomerang, swung himself over the side of the cockpit and fastened the seat harness. The aircraft had been on the flight line all day and despite a shade canvas strung over the area, the cockpit was like an oven—almost every piece of exposed metal was hot to the touch. He made the pre-start checks, primed the engine then after signalling the ground crew, hit the starter.

The Pratt & Whitney coughed, then swung into life. After a minute's idle, Masters checked the magnetos, engine temperatures and pressures, then waved the chocks away. Tail waggling as he ruddered the aircraft side to side, he taxied from the revetment, wheels bumping over the steel-plank tarmac. A green light winked from the little wooden control tower and he swung onto the runway.

Pressing hard on the brakes, Masters dragged the stick back into his stomach and opened the throttle. The engine responded, the propeller whipping dust into a swirling tornado behind the aircraft. He glanced in the cockpit mirror to see it engulf a group of soldiers walking near the end of the strip, blowing one of them into a ditch that had filled with water from a recent rain shower.

Masters smiled as he backed off the power. He hadn't meant to catch them, but the temptation was always there when the opportunity arose. What he really wanted was to get some air flowing around him. He was slowly roasting; already his shirt was darkened by sweat.

A quick instrument check confirmed all was okay, so he released the brakes, gradually opened the throttle and allowed the aircraft to gain speed. Then, juggling rudder and stick, he lifted the tail, pushed the throttle to take-off power while easing in more rudder to counter the engine's torque. The whine of rubber on steel ceased as the wheels left the runway. He allowed the speed to build, then pulled the undercarriage retract lever and hauled back the stick. Relieved of drag, the aircraft surged ahead, climbing eagerly. At 300 feet he crossed the upwind threshold, then began a sweeping right turn that took him out over the sea until he was heading south-east parallel to the coast.

Continuing the climb, he levelled at 3000 feet and eased the throttle to cruising speed. At this altitude the air was cooler and he left the canopy open. Ahead the water shimmered in the afternoon sun, the coast a white-fringed green strip. Inland, heavy cumulus clouds were building over the mountains.

Today's sortie followed a route Masters had flown many times. Staying over the water a few miles off the coast, it would take twenty-five minutes to reach Muschu Island. His mission was to reconnoitre the island and attract the attention of the survivors of the Z Special patrol—if there were any. That meant going in low and slow.

It could be risky; however, the Japanese knew the Boomerang was a reconnaissance aircraft and firing on it would immediately compromise their position. It was also strongly built and could absorb a tremendous amount of damage, so the chances of a first-round kill were low. With four machine guns and two 20 mm cannons he could make life miserable for any challengers, so the odds were in his favour.

A pity, really. Sometimes it was easier to allow an impatient Jap to take a shot at him and give the game away, rather than have to stooge around staring at endless jungle for hours. He could then call in air support or see if a broadside of 20 mm cannon and .303 rounds changed their attitude. The only real worry was those bastards with the 30 mm Oerlikons—one squirt from them in the right place and he'd be a puff of smoke. But staying low was the secret: travelling only a few metres above the trees gave most gunners only a fleeting glimpse of the aircraft.

Today's sortie, however, wasn't to find the enemy. If they did fire at him, he'd be reluctant to shoot back in case there were friendlies around.

After fifteen minutes he saw a white streak on the water heading south off to his left. Selecting channel six on the high-frequency radio, he thumbed the transmit button and made a quick call. The answer was immediate, the codeword reply confirming that it was HDML 1321 on its way to Muschu. He considered giving them a quick fly-by, but decided now wasn't the time for theatrics. He needed to conserve fuel—this could be a long sortie.

Ten minutes later he sighted Muschu and Kairiru Islands, deceptively beautiful in the afternoon sun. He flew down the middle of the strait between the two islands, then east of Muschu he climbed and circled slowly while searching the sea for the Fairmile. It had been 30 kilometres offshore all day, but should now be heading into a position closer to the island. He sighted it in his two o'clock position about 15 kilometres east of Muschu, heading towards the island. Again using channel six, he made a call and received the correct acknowledgment. He checked his knee pad where the mission sequences, call signs and codenames were listed.

So far so good.

The Fairmile had received the mission brief via encrypted radio and understood what they had to do. They would be just out of sight to anyone on Muschu, yet close enough for an inshore dash and rescue if he could find any patrol survivors. It would be bloody dangerous, but the Fairmile could lay down a hefty covering barrage with its Oerlikons, Bofors and machine guns. Meanwhile he could keep the Japanese occupied and deal with any unexpected intruders. And if the timing was right, HDML 1321 would be joining the party in a few hours.

It sounded like a workable plan.

Tapping the fuel gauge, Masters saw he had enough for two hours on station, maybe more. That would give him sufficient fuel for the return flight, plus a small reserve in case of bad weather. He glanced at the mainland. The clouds were still building over the mountains, but along the coast the sky remained clear.

Okay, it's time for the show, he thought. Tightening his harness, he made a pre-action check, then slid the canopy shut.

He flew west of Muschu, then putting the sun behind him, rolled into a steep dive. Opening the throttle, speed built quickly and soon exceeded 300 knots. Altimeter unwinding, he aimed at the western end of the island. At an altitude of 1000 feet, he began pulling back on the stick. He felt the G forces coming on as he levelled from the dive 150 feet above the trees and streaked over the middle of the island, engine howling and supercharger whistling. Flashing over the hills at the eastern end, he hauled back the stick and climbed vertically. He snap-rolled the little aircraft, counted one, two, three clockwise rotations, paused, then reversed the roll. One, two, three.

He flipped inverted, pulled through, then tucked back down into another dive, this time at half-throttle. Again he howled low over the trees, then allowing speed to wash off, began a wide circuit out over the southern coast.

Masters was thoroughly enjoying himself. For an aircraft someone once described as being built from spare parts, baling wire and Golden Syrup tins, the Boomerang was a bloody marvel. It might not be the world's greatest fighter, but it was manoeuvrable, strong and very, very noisy. By now every Jap on the island would be aware that he was around, and hopefully, too, were the Z Special blokes.

Lowering flaps and flying at 100 knots, he pulled open the canopy then dropped to tree-top level. Passing over the eastern tip of the island, he followed the beach around to the western end, then circled out to sea and repeated his track. It was against his instincts to be predictable, but in this case he knew the risk was justified. If the patrol was down there, they had to be able to get into a position to signal him. As he flew, his left hand rested on the throttle, ready to shove it wide open at the first hint of ground fire.

He varied his course slightly, flew along the northern coast and circled the western end of the island, sighting huts and buildings obviously used by the Japanese which he noted on his knee pad. They'd get the treatment later from Seven Squadron's Beauforts.

For two hours he kept up the routine, circling, diving, varying the engine speed, and generally making a nuisance of himself. Once he flew so low along the beach on the southern coast he feared a well-aimed coconut could bring him down. But nothing happened—even circling over Muschu Bay, where it was known the enemy had their main HQ, failed to evoke a response. Nor were there any signals from the patrol: no mirror flashes, Verey flares, smoke—nothing.

As a last gesture, with fuel low, he made a slow run up the middle of the island, blipping out V for Victory in Morse by varying the engine note. If the patrol were down there it would give them encouragement. If not, then perhaps it could be considered their epitaph.

Throttling up, he headed east at 300 feet and, 10 kilometres out, passed over the Fairmile, wings rocking. They acknowledged with two long flashes on the Aldis lamp, then he banked away and set course for Tadji.

The Fairmile went about and headed north. Low on fuel, they'd replenish at Aitape and remain on stand-by. Maybe HDML 1321 would have better luck tonight.

36. PNG MAINLAND:

18 APRIL, 1600 HOURS

Dennis had found an unused track winding north and he'd made good progress. For the last hour he'd climbed steadily into high country, the jungle thinning to rainforest crowded with ferns. At the top of a hill, the track ran through a grassy clearing and, pausing beside a tree, he checked it before crossing.

The sun was casting long shadows and the air was still. Already a fine mist was starting to form as a chill descended. It was quiet, the trees unmoving, just a few distant bird calls echoing in the valleys nearby. Cautiously he moved along the track, then stopped.

About 20 metres away to his left, among thick ferns he discerned the outline of a small hut. It had been well camouflaged and it took him a few moments to see it among all the shadows. It looked as if it hadn't been used for some time, but he remained still, carefully checking out the surrounding area. Seeing nothing he moved quietly across the clearing.

Suddenly a voice shouted and he saw three Japanese near the hut. They'd been lying on the ground and were now scrambling to their feet.

One raised his rifle, but before he could fire, Dennis squeezed off a quick burst from his Sten that caught the soldier across the chest. He fell on his face, rifle discharging as he hit the ground. Instead of fighting, the others turned and fled into the forest. Dennis caught one of them with another burst and he dropped. The other dodged around a tree, bark chipping near his head as Dennis swung the Sten on him. Shrieking loudly, he vanished into the foliage followed by another stream of 9 mm rounds.

As two more soldiers appeared from the far side of the clearing, Dennis turned and bolted, making for the track where it dropped down the side of the hill. Bullets snapped overhead as he slipped and skidded to the bottom where he splashed through a creek, then scrambled up the other side into heavy undergrowth. He climbed until he could go no further, then crawled into a clump of bushes under a tree. He was near exhaustion and sat chest heaving, wondering how much longer he could keep this up. Far behind he could still hear shooting. Gradually it lessened, then stopped.

For ten minutes he rested, listening for the Japanese, but there was no more firing on the hill. He checked his weapon. He'd used more than half a magazine in the last encounter, which left him with about 70 rounds. Removing the magazine he worked the Sten's bolt—it was still moving smoothly, but it would need cleaning soon. Without oil, that would be a problem. He released the bolt, then replaced the magazine with a full one. At least with the action closed it would limit moisture entry around the mechanism. Again he wished for an Owen gun and cursed the Pommie bastard who'd designed the Sten.

Deciding to stay away from the track, he began climbing, forcing himself through the undergrowth, his feet slipping as the hill steepened. It took almost an hour of exhausting effort to reach the top, then scrambling on his knees onto a grassy knoll, he lay near a fallen tree until he'd recovered.

From here he could see the coast about 6 kilometres away, and beyond to the south-east were Muschu and Kairiru Islands. It was a strange feeling being able to see the islands, and it was almost hard to believe he'd actually crossed the strait and made it this far.

Resisting the temptation to stay longer, he moved off the knoll and headed north along a broad ridge line, remaining in high undergrowth and travelling parallel to a nearby track. For almost an hour he continued, then with the sun low in the sky, he began searching for somewhere to hole up for the night.

He'd just found a thick clump of ferns that looked perfect when he heard voices nearby. Crouching behind the ferns, he saw a Japanese patrol approaching along the track. There were eight of them, well spaced and looking more disciplined than those he'd seen so far. They passed by so close he could have reached out and touched them.

Deciding that the lay-up he'd found was too near a patrol route, he waited five minutes then crossed the track, headed into the scrub and descended the hill. Here the jungle opened out into a small flat valley, with huts scattered among gardens. It looked deserted, but he resisted the temptation to raid the gardens for food. Slowly he crept around the perimeter, then stepped into cover when he heard voices ahead.

From a hut only a few metres away, a Japanese soldier stepped out cradling a small child. He sat on a log and played with the child, bouncing it on his knee and lifting it high. For half an hour the soldier played, the child running, laughing and clapping, then lunging into the soldier's arms. Dennis watched, unable to move in case the soldier saw him. If he did, Dennis would have no choice but to open fire on him, which would probably kill the child as well. Not a pleasant thought, but a choice he'd have to make. Fortunately a Papuan woman appeared at the hut door and called. Lifting the child onto his shoulders, the soldier went back into the hut and shut the door.

Dennis moved on, skirting the village. Once clear, he climbed up the opposite side of the valley onto a plateau covered in rainforest. There he found a perfect hide between the fern-covered buttress roots of a huge tree. As the last rays of the sun seeped through the canopy, he removed his gear and settled down for the night.

37. MUSCHU ISLAND:

18 APRIL, 2000 HOURS

HDML 1321 reached Muschu after a six-hour run from Aitape, the engineer coaxing almost 15 knots from the twin diesels. The sea was calm and they made good time, passing the eastern tip of Kairiru Island at sunset, then standing off over the horizon until last light. That night the moon was a quarter-disc on the western horizon, partly hidden by cloud. The moon's diffused glow was enough to make the ship visible when they were close in to shore, so Lieutenant Palmer waited until the moon was low over the mainland before heading closer to Muschu.

At 2130 hours they sighted Muschu's silhouette on the horizon. After taking a compass bearing to the island, Palmer ordered the speed reduced to 6 knots, then went to the chart table and examined his map. With the moon low in the west, the island cast a long shadow from the eastern tip that should allow them to approach Cape Saum without being seen. Later, when the moon set, he'd patrol along the southern coast. The tide was on the rise, so he figured he'd be able to get close enough for the patrol survivors to hail the boat from the shore.

It would still be risky, and there was a very real danger they'd be seen by the Japanese—but even if they were, there was little the enemy could do. While it was known they had heavy machine guns along some coastal areas, they would probably be reluctant to reveal their positions for fear of retribution later. However, if they did open up, his gunners would return fire and he'd be ready with the throttles. They'd done this many times on coastal raids and Palmer knew how to make his boat a difficult target when necessary. It was a risk the crew was prepared to take.

The heavy guns could be a problem though. Palmer knew the capabilities of the Japanese 140. Copied from a British Vickers design, it was a damned good weapon, accurate and quick firing. Manned by an efficient crew it could punch out six rounds a minute, and in close they'd be using open sights—lining the ship up in the crosshairs like a duck in a shooting gallery.

In the red glow of the map light, Palmer examined the suspected location of the guns. On a low hill about 30 metres above sea level, they commanded a broad arc covering the southern coastal area of the island, and were well placed to cause big problems to the landing force in Wewak Harbour. He could understand why the Army was concerned: he'd seen the damage a 140 mm shell could do. Against the steel hull of a warship it wasn't pretty. Against an HDML's wooden construction the result would be catastrophic. But as the Sixth Division's Intelligence Officer had suggested, if the Japanese were preparing the guns for the defence of Wewak, they weren't about to sacrifice them by exposing their position to sink one Australian patrol boat.

Even so, he'd be taking a big risk by bringing the boat so close to shore—the Japanese might find it too tempting not to try a quick shot or two. Taking a sheet of paper from the log pad, Palmer overlayed the map and traced the shoreline. Marking the distances and contours, he made a quick calculation. Then he pencilled his proposed course around the island on the map plot. Satisfied, he tapped the First Officer's shoulder, pointed to the map and explained that tonight they had to remain inside the line he'd drawn.

The First Officer raised his eyebrows and shrugged. If the skipper wanted to commit suicide then so be it.

Palmer flipped off the map light, lifted his binoculars and scanned the island's brooding silhouette. They'd soon find out whether Six Division's theory was correct.

In the ship's radio shack, Major Cardew sat on a cramped seat beside the radio operator, listening to the hollow crackle and hiss of atmospherics. There was still hope that the patrol would suddenly radio in, and he willed their signal to break through the clutter of background noise. But the closer they drew to Muschu, the quieter the radios seemed to become. The patrol's ATR4 sets were capable of transmitting for hundreds of miles, so he knew it wasn't a matter of range. Even the little SCR36 walkie-talkies were capable of a range of 10 kilometres or more at night over water.

Cardew was beginning to face the inevitable prospect that all the patrol were dead or the survivors had been captured. The loss of eight men was a severe blow to a small unit like the SRD. Sure they'd lost men before—too many times—but eight would be the biggest loss they'd taken since Operation Rimau. April wasn't shaping up as the best of months for Z Special—Department Three had already notified two men lost in Java, and it was suspected another patrol was in trouble in Borneo. He could sympathise with their commanders. Like him, they'd be doing everything they could to rescue their men and spending the time in between anguishing about whether there was something they could have done to prepare them better. At the end of it all would be an investigation, not so much to pin blame, but hopefully to learn from the experience to better equip or train the next patrol. Ironically, with the war nearing an end, he wondered if the lessons learned would survive, or if they would be confined to a musty archive, never to be seen again.

Removing his headset, Cardew leaned back and rubbed a hand through his hair. He was tired. The last six days had been a bitch, but he reminded himself it probably amounted to nothing compared with what the men of Operation Copper had endured.

He needed some fresh air. Leaving the radio shack he headed for the companionway.

■ ■ ■

Lieutenant Palmer had timed the approach to the island perfectly. The moon was now totally hidden by cloud, with just a diffused glow lighting the western sky. He'd brought the ship in to half a mile off Sup Point and could feel the swell beginning to rise as the water shallowed. Cardew had joined him on the bridge and together through binoculars they strained to see the shoreline. Here the land was in total shadow, and they could barely make out the white water as the waves foamed low over the reef. They could smell the island—a conflicting cocktail of perfumes and pungent odours that both delighted and repelled.

Palmer eased the boat north towards Cape Saum, venturing closer to the shore until they were less than 100 metres from the reef. He was navigating by feel, measuring every swell as it passed under the boat by the way it moved, ready to power up and head away at the slightest hint of the back-drag from a big wave. It was here that the patrol's first rendezvous had been scheduled for the night of 12 April, but they'd not made it. So why would they now? It was a question both men left unasked for fear of having to answer.

For almost an hour they remained, engines softly idling, standing watch and willing the foldboats to materialise from the darkness. Below, the rum-laced coffee was waiting. It would be bad luck not to have it ready. The radio operator strained at his headphones, radios tuned, listening to the empty hiss and crackle of atmospherics. Even the engineer, standing between the slowly turning diesels, waited anxiously for the order to power up that would tell him the men were safe. All reached out, praying for a miracle.

None came.

By 0100 hours the glow from the moon had vanished and the night was now inky black. Palmer decided to shift position. This meant rounding Cape Barabar and coming into the gun battery's line of fire. He turned and looked at Cardew. In the dim red combat light, his face remained mask-like, jaw clenched.

Palmer checked the plot again, flicked off the combat light, then gave the order. The helmsman swung the wheel as the engines throttled up. HDML 1321 went about and headed slowly west. Against the backdrop of stars, Cape Barabar was a low, black finger jutting from the coast. Palmer sighted on the cape, then instructed the helmsman to alter course ten degrees to port. He'd swing wide around the point to avoid the reef, then tuck in close to the beach and hug the coast. Hands gripping the bridge coaming, he steadied himself as the ship rose to a big wave that passed underneath, then foamed in towards the shore. In years to come, the point would become a mecca for surfers, but that night the waves were a curse, capable of broaching the boat if they hit beam-on.

They rounded Cape Barabar into a calmer patch of water. Altering course towards the shore, Palmer carefully felt his way closer, then turned to run parallel with the reef.

Through the binoculars he could see the beach and beyond it, the hill where the guns were reported to be hidden. He gauged the range, then glanced at the map plot. They were less than 500 metres from the guns. If the Japs were going to fire on them, now would be the time.

Slowly they cruised past, all eyes fixed on the hill. Then it was astern and Palmer smiled thinly. What he hadn't told Cardew was that the British Vickers 140 mm naval gun wasn't capable of depressing its barrel more than six degrees. If the Japanese had copied the design faithfully then they'd have the same limitations. According to his calculations, from their position on the hill they couldn't bring the weapons to bear on a target closer than 2 kilometres.

For the next three hours HDML 1321 cruised the southern coast of Muschu, then as the first greying of dawn tinged the eastern sky, Palmer slipped north around Cape Barabar, powered up and left the island in their wake.

38. PNG MAINLAND:

19 APRIL, 0600 HOURS

Screeching filled his ears. Dennis snapped awake. For a moment panic swept him, but he forced his fear aside. Gripping the Sten in his right hand, he curled his finger lightly on the trigger as he slowly raised the weapon. He remained silent, his mind focusing as he drove the fatigue from his brain. Like a radio tuning to a distant station, he sifted through the sounds that assaulted him like a living thing, trying to make sense of the noise. Then he recognised it. In the trees around him, hundreds of birds were joining in a raucous chorus that was spreading like ripples through the forest. Dawn was approaching and through the canopy of leaves, he could see the sky turning pink.

Exhaling slowly, he remained mouth open in a position that peaked his hearing, listening for anything that indicated the Japanese were near. The only sounds were the birds, now competing with each other for the loudest and noisiest call. In a way it was comforting, for he knew if they sensed danger, they'd fall silent.

Maybe.

His thoughts drifted. For a moment he allowed himself the luxury of remembering home . . .

Wake up!

He forced his eyes open. The birds were quieter now, their calls less frenzied, as if an argument had been settled and they were discussing a few minor details. The sky was a vivid red, the sun streaming through the canopy and dappling the leafy jungle floor. Already the chill of night was lifting and he felt the humidity pressing in like a heavy blanket.

An insect buzzed.

Carefully, with his back to the tree, his right hand gripping the Sten, he used his left hand to part the palm fronds he'd used for cover. For a moment he was reluctant to leave the tree's buttressed roots, the hideaway suddenly comforting and warm. Like a kid hiding under the blankets in a storm.

God I'm hungry, he thought. And thirsty. A beer, I'd give anything for a beer. Or tea, hot and sweet. Better still, coffee, strong and black . . .

Wake up!

His eyes snapped open. Slowly he stood, keeping his back against the tree. His body ached, his legs tingled as the circulation returned. His head felt as if it was stuffed with cotton wool.

How long was it now? Seven days, eight? He'd slept maybe two hours each night. In training they'd been taught the effects of sleep deprivation, being kept awake for more than three days without a break. After that, strange things happened. Hallucinations, falling asleep standing up, falling asleep walking. Some people ran about gibbering. Others just glazed over and sat speechless like zombies. It was insidious.

Last night he'd slept little. It had rained almost continually, and when it didn't rain the mosquitoes had found him. The best he could do was rest, eyes closed and shivering. In some ways it was more exhausting than running all day.

Should've brought some of doc's magic pills with me, he thought.

He scanned the area, his weapon following his gaze. The rainforest was a maze of trees and ferns, with shafts of sunlight breaking the shadows. After taking a long drink from his canteen, he rummaged in his pack for the remaining glucose tablet. He munched slowly, trying to savour the taste while avoiding thoughts of other food, then washed it down with water.

He made a quick body check, noting that the coral gashes on his legs were healing well. Probably the swim, he thought—salt water does wonders. Also the soft skin around his eyes where the mosquitoes had feasted had lost most of its swelling—again probably due to the salt water. He knew he should check his feet, but decided against it. If he removed his boots his feet could swell and he'd never get them on again. At the moment, although they were sore from days of walking, they felt fine.

After taking off what remained of his shirt, he saw that he was covered with scratches and cuts, some looking red and angry. A vine slash on his upper left arm was the worst, so he used a little of his remaining water to clean it. Digging into his pack, he took out his first aid kit, found the antiseptic cream and smeared it on the wound. He ripped a length of gauze from a field dressing and bound the arm, taking care not to wrap it too tightly.

That was about all he could do. He considered himself lucky to be only scratched and bruised after almost a week on the run. All it would take was a twisted ankle and he'd be in serious trouble . . .

I'm not in serious trouble now? he thought. Half the bloody Japanese Army is after me . . .

He looked at his shirt. It was a dirt-smeared, shredded rag. Ironically it actually helped camouflage him by breaking up his outline.

Must look a fright, he thought, rubbing a hand over his stubbled face. I need a shave, a hot shower, then a good feed . . .

And sleep . . .

He shrugged on his shirt then paused, making doubly sure that no one was near, for the next part of his routine would leave him very vulnerable.

With the dexterity of experience, he quickly removed the magazine from his Sten, then stripped the weapon to its working components. Despite yesterday's cleaning they were already showing signs of rust.

Always the bloody way, Dennis thought. For some reason military weapons were made from steel that was prone to rust. He was sure it was intended to keep idle soldiers busy. So how to clean it without oil?

His cleaning rag still had a trace of oil left, so he used it to wipe away as much rust as he could, only paying attention to the essential moving parts. The barrel was clear—it probably needed a quick pull-through, but that could wait. It wouldn't affect the weapon's accuracy in close-up fighting.

Parts of the exterior were covered with fine rust. Externally it could rust into oblivion for all he cared. It made no difference to how the weapon functioned.

He needed oil. But from where?

Turning to his medical kit he found the antiseptic cream and squeezed a little of the yellow ointment onto his finger. It was thicker than oil and smelled faintly of fish. But it was better than nothing. He rubbed it on the bolt and smeared it thinly on the spring and inside the bolt receiver.

Next he emptied the magazine of rounds and stripped it. He removed the spring, then stretched it a little to restore its power. After cleaning and coating all parts lightly with ointment, he reassembled the magazine. Laying out the remaining 60 rounds on his pack, he inspected and cleaned them one by one. Had salt water seeped into the cordite and left them useless? Except for a slight greening of the brass groove that surrounded the percussion caps, they seemed okay. Experience told him they would be fine, yet there remained a nagging doubt. He wouldn't know until he pulled the trigger.

He assembled the weapon, worked the bolt to and fro. Although a little stiff, it moved smoothly. After reloading his remaining rounds then replacing the magazine, he leaned the Sten against the tree.

Now he had to think through his next move. He needed water. There were plenty of streams around and all he had to do was make sure he collected some water from a spot not being watched by the Japanese. That could be a problem. Best way was to find a stream overhung by foliage, crawl on his belly to the edge, reach out and fill his canteen. Hopefully an arm and canteen would be difficult to see.

Unfolding his map, he oriented it with his compass. The map told him precious little except that he was in thick rainforest on hilly terrain cut by creeks that ran out to the sea. Since landing, he estimated he'd travelled about 6 kilometres inland and almost 20 north. A rough guess suggested he was about 10, maybe 15 kilometres south of the Australian line of advance.

A twig breaking made him catch his breath. Was it his imagination? He folded the map away then listened, senses tingling.

The sound came again, this time a soft rustling of leaves from somewhere behind the tree. Reaching for the Sten, he gently drew back the bolt with one hand while covering the bolt receiver with the other to muffle the click of the trigger sear engaging. Pressing hard into the tree he held the weapon ready, remaining still, head raised to see over the buttressed roots either side.

He noticed with a chill that the birds had all fallen silent.

How long had it been like that?

He cursed himself for allowing his attention to wander.

A swish of leaves, closer now. Then a shadow, long and distorted by motes of sun, moving over the forest floor to his right. Dennis slowly swung the Sten towards it.

A figure came into his peripheral vision. A small yellow head, atop a long, thick, blue neck . . .

What the hell is that?

A bird! Almost six feet tall, strutting on long, powerful legs with a heavy, penguin-shaped body covered with shiny black feathers. Its head was topped by a bony, helmet-like crest.

A cassowary.

They'd been warned about them. Capable of tearing a man apart with their talons, cassowaries were aggressively territorial. Known to attack without provocation, the Papuans regarded killing them as a right of passage for young warriors. Wearing their feathers was a symbol of power among many tribes.

The cassowary moved past about 4 metres to his right. Almost the size of an ostrich, it looked fiercely prehistoric. It suddenly stopped as if sensing something. Its head snapped around and beady eyes met his.

Cautiously it took a step towards him. Dennis could see its three-clawed feet, the dagger-like middle talons almost six inches long. It took another step, this time with confidence. It took another, then paused 2 metres away, one foot raised, the gleaming talon pointing at him in an accusing fashion.

It lunged.

He squeezed the Sten's trigger.

Two rounds cracked out, slammed into the bird and it dropped twitching in a cloud of feathers.

Dennis was on his feet, slinging his pack over his shoulder, leaping over the carcass while the shots still echoed around him. He bolted, dodging vines and weaving around trees. After 50 metres he broke right, travelled another 50 metres, then paused, crouching near a clump of ferns. Heart pounding, he listened to the sounds of the jungle. It was deathly still.

He was shocked by the fear the cassowary had evoked. There was something strangely primal about being attacked by an animal.

It was only an overgrown budgerigar, he reassured himself. Should've stopped and taken a drumstick. Be good roasted over a fire . . .

Again he forced his mind to stop wandering.

He feared the Japanese would have heard the shots. But would they follow? It was difficult to judge direction and distance in heavy foliage, and there were often small enemy groups out hunting food. They might assume the shots came from their own.

The best thing was to assume nothing. If they were after him they'd soon show themselves. Should he move now or wait? If he surprised them maybe he could nail them all . . . but . . .

He checked the weapon, removed the magazine and worked the bolt. It felt smoother. The heat of firing maybe? It seemed antiseptic cream made a good lubricant. He thought about passing the tip on when he got back. *If* he got back.

High in the trees nearby a bird shrieked, a whooping howl that was answered from a long way off.

He decided that no one was following. Noting the angle of the sun through the canopy, he figured it was about 0700 hours. Already he was sweating. The insects were out in force now, buzzing around looking for flesh to feed on. He slapped at a huge fly that settled on his wrist. It zipped away with impunity and circled before landing on a nearby branch and peering down at him with bulging eyes.

He stared back.

If the Japs don't get you the bloody insects will.

On the ground among the detritus, he could see leeches waving their heads in rhythmic patterns as they sought the heat from his body. A few were making their way towards him.

He shuddered.

Forget them. A bullet will kill you quicker . . .

Using his compass, he found a distant tree that was almost due north and set off, walking at a brisk pace. Reaching the tree, he paused to rest, then took another bearing and repeated the procedure. For a while travelling through the rainforest was relatively easy, the terrain undulating, with large trees and only a light undergrowth of ferns and plants. Even so he found he was tiring quickly and his rest breaks were becoming longer.

He had to find somewhere to hole up and sleep. If he kept going like this he knew he'd make mistakes. He was already making them—the last bearing he'd taken was thirty degrees out and he'd had to backtrack to compensate. Any more of that and he'd wind up going around in circles.

Pushing himself on, the rainforest gave way to heavily wooded country cut by steep-banked streams. Crossing them was an effort: sliding down one bank and splashing through the water to scramble up the slippery bank on the other side taxed his strength until he could go no further. He rested, drank the last of his water, then pushed on to the next creek where he refilled his canteen.

The terrain was now rising and he found a narrow track that wound back up into the rainforest. Slowly he climbed, forcing one step after another, feet slipping as the track steepened. Sweat stinging his eyes, he tried to see ahead, but found himself constantly looking down, searching for footholds as the trail became almost vertical. Clutching vines and tree roots, he struggled to reach the top, where the terrain opened out into broad grassland. Again he rested, taking a quick mouthful of water.

He was about to move off again when he heard Japanese voices ahead. Easing off the track and crouching in heavy undergrowth, he waited as the voices approached. He flicked off the Sten's safety catch and aimed the weapon. Through the foliage he could see along the track to a bend. The voices were louder now, chattering excitedly.

Four soldiers appeared, rifles slung over their shoulders. They passed by so close he could have reached out and touched them. He watched them go, still talking and laughing.

Where there were four well-fed, well-armed Japanese there'd undoubtedly be more. But he had no choice: the further inland he went, the more difficult the terrain was; head towards the coast and he'd run into more Japs. Straight up the middle was the only way.

He moved on, more cautious now, the track winding through an area of thick kunai grass. For almost an hour he continued at a steady pace, stopping regularly to listen. Coming to a rise with a clear field of vision to the coast, he concealed himself and was about to take compass bearings to fix his position when he heard the distinctive scratch of artillery rounds passing overhead to the north.

The shells slammed into a hill about 3 kilometres away. He watched the barrage, counting the impacts and hoping they were on target. For almost ten minutes the firing continued, then it stopped, leaving the hill covered in drifting grey smoke.

The artillery gave him encouragement. They looked like 25-pounders and with a maximum range of about 14 kilometres, it meant he was getting very close to the Australian line of advance. Now he had to be even more cautious—it would be the ultimate irony to be shot by an advancing Australian patrol.

Draining his canteen, he set out again. The track was now heading north and for ten minutes he made quick progress. Then suddenly, after coming around a bend, he came head-on to another patrol. This one was moving quietly, weapons ready, well spread out. Before they could react he opened fire, hitting the leader in the chest. The others scattered either side of the track as Dennis shifted targets and fired a long burst that slashed the kunai grass around them.

Changing magazines, Dennis fired again, then leapt into the grass on his right, ran 20 metres, stopped and crouched beside a tree.

The Japanese were now firing in his direction, bullets cracking overhead, a few chipping bark off the tree. Dennis remained in cover, listening to the confusion, trying to work out their positions. Most of them were to his left, about 30 metres away. They were still firing, but it was more coordinated now and he realised from the shouted orders that someone had taken charge and they were forming an extended line intending to sweep through his position.

Silently he backed off through the tall grass towards the edge of the hill, then paused. The firing had stopped and he could hear movement as the enemy regrouped.

How many were there? He'd confronted four, but he'd glimpsed others further down the track. Probably a squad, maybe a dozen.

Suddenly behind him he heard the grass rustle. He turned slowly. Ten metres away the top of the kunai quivered. Someone was trying to outflank him. Crouching low, Dennis checked his Sten, pushing his thumb into the ejector port onto the cartridges in the magazine to make sure they were still feeding. The rounds moved smoothly and, reassured, he slowly raised the weapon.

To his front about 20 metres off he could hear the rest of the squad, their footsteps now in parade-ground unison, a steady thump and swish that grew louder as they advanced. He knew their battle drill—they'd be in extended line 2 metres apart, rifles level and bayonets fixed. Meanwhile, from one of his flanks, he could expect covering fire at any moment. He'd be pinned and they'd overrun him. He didn't stand a chance.

So where was their fire support? The grass to his right only 5 metres away moved. He heard the click of metal. A machine gun being readied? So close? Twisting slowly, Dennis aimed the Sten. The grass shook again and through it he saw the boots and trousers of a Japanese soldier. Sighting above the man's belt, Dennis squeezed off three rounds. The soldier groaned and dropped.

Dennis leapt to his feet, scrambled over the side of the hill, rolled once, then bouncing up onto his feet, slid and scrambled down the slope. Firing erupted behind him, but it went high and wide. Reaching the bottom of the hill, he splashed through a creek, clambered up the opposite slope then rolled under a clump of bushes and lay gasping.

A sharp pain stabbed through his stomach. Looking down, he saw his shirt was covered in blood. For a moment he thought he'd been wounded, but then he realised with relief that the blood was caused by slashes from the thorny vines he'd forced his way through.

He took a quick drink from his canteen, then lay listening to the sounds around him. The Japanese were still firing sporadically, but the shots sounded as if they were moving away. After five minutes they stopped completely. For another ten minutes Dennis rested, then knowing if he remained too long he'd never get going again, he crawled from his hiding place and dragged himself up the hill until he reached the crest.

There he found another track heading north, so he paused, checked the area, then set out again. He had to put as much distance between him and the last contact as possible. The problem was he appeared to be in a concentration of Japanese troops reacting to the Australian advance.

For another hour he continued, the track eventually winding down into a valley. He'd neither seen nor heard any more Japanese so he decided to rest. Moving off the track he found a lay-up in a grove of trees. From the sun's position he judged it was almost midday. He'd give himself an hour, then hopefully he'd be able to reach the Australian positions by sundown.

39. SIXTH DIVISION HQ, AITAPE:

19 APRIL, 1300 HOURS

Heavy rain was falling when HDML 1321 motored into Aitape Harbour. The boat nudged into the jetty; the diesels gave a short burst of reverse power, then faded. The deckhands cinched the lines to the bollards and the hull eased onto the fenders, jetty timbers creaking. Major Cardew climbed through the forward companionway hatch, glanced up at the bridge and tipped his cap in farewell. On the bridge, Lieutenant Palmer responded. The two men looked at each other for a moment, then Cardew hurried along the deck and jumped ashore.

A jeep waited at the end of the jetty. He splashed over to it and climbed in. The drive to Sixth Division HQ was slow, the jeep slipping on the muddy road, wipers slapping futilely against the tropical downpour that hammered against the canvas roof and sides. Beside him the driver tried to make conversation, but Cardew remained silent, deep in thought.

Already he was working on ways to improve the next patrol—it looked as if they'd have to try Muschu again, irrespective of the risk. What had they learned from Operation Copper? Not much. But he wanted to do it better next time.

One area for improvement was communications. Although the patrol had gone completely off the air, there was a possibility it was due to radio failure. He knew it was a remote chance for all sets to go at once, but the radios used were notoriously susceptible to water damage, especially the ATR4. It was an old design, originally intended for bushfire services in Australia—not military work. The Americans were producing some new compact, powerful radios, which was exactly what they needed. He'd applied for them almost six months ago, but they'd been given the run-around by the Defence Department in Canberra and he was still being plagued with questions from public servants as to why existing equipment wasn't suitable.

Weapons? Maybe they needed more firepower—there wasn't a soldier on earth who wouldn't welcome more. There were plenty of alternatives, including the Browning 9 mm automatic pistol to replace the faithful Smith & Wesson revolver. The Owen gun could replace the Sten—why the Special Operations Executive insisted on keeping the British weapon he didn't know. Some very impressive automatic assault rifles were now being used by the German Wehrmacht in Europe—last-minute developments that thankfully were now too late to make a difference to the outcome of this war, but an indication of what the future held.

A major difficulty was patrol extraction, especially in an emergency. Insertion wasn't that much of a problem, almost anything could be used to get in: patrol boats, submarines, foldboats, swimming—whatever suited the situation. It was getting back out when the enemy were fully alerted that was difficult. It was then that a quick response time was essential for survival.

On the run back to Aitape he'd discussed the problem with Palmer. Cardew had suggested that if SRD was considering going back to Muschu then they should be based closer. Vokeo Island could provide a good forward base. There were no Japanese there and it was only a couple of hours from Muschu or Wewak. Put a detachment on the island—it didn't have to be anything elaborate, just men, tents, supplies and a good radio setup. Palmer agreed: he knew the island and there were sheltered bays where the HDML could anchor.

The more Cardew thought about the idea, the more he liked it.

Even so, the reaction time for an emergency extraction could still be too slow. Patrol boats had to remain out of sight during the day, and even the fastest torpedo launches could be seen approaching for almost twenty minutes or more. Parking a submarine off the coast was one option, but subs were scarce resources, rarely able to devote time to small operations.

In Europe they were using aircraft with short take-off and landing capabilities to get their agents in and out. That was hard to do in the Pacific with everything covered with thick jungle, but it had potential. In Java and Timor, Section Three were already using PBY seaplanes successfully.

The list went on. There had to be better ways of doing everything. After the war, someone needed the foresight to sit down and objectively examine the use of special operations. There was still entrenched prejudice against them by many senior officers, who seemed more concerned with preserving their traditional empires than winning the war. The concept was proven: special operations could yield results that far outweighed their costs, both material and human.

The key to it all, however, was the quality of those men willing to risk their lives in such ventures. Now he had to account for eight of the best. Unfortunately, he couldn't write those compassionate, descriptive letters that had become so fashionable lately. As much as he wanted to, the truth of their deaths had to wait until the war was over. Until then their loved ones would have to be content with the harsh reality of cliched wording on Commonwealth letterhead and perhaps a visit from the padre.

They deserved better, Cardew thought.

Cardew failed to notice that the jeep had stopped outside the Sixth Division HQ. The driver was looking at him wondering whether the major's damp face was caused by yet another bloody leak in the jeep's canvas roof.

40. PNG MAINLAND:

19 APRIL, 1400 HOURS

Dennis rested, dozing lightly, to be woken after an hour by approaching aircraft. A flight of three Beauforts flew up the valley so low he could see the pilots and for a moment he was tempted to try to attract their attention. Realising the futility of doing so, he watched them disappear towards Wewak, their engines echoing from the hills around him. Stiffly he got to his feet. His body ached in a dozen places and a wave of nausea swept him. He shivered and for a moment feared he was coming down with malaria, but then realised it had rained while he slept and he was soaking wet.

The dizziness slowly passed. He checked his Sten by working the bolt with the magazine off to spread the remaining grease through the mechanism. It was stiff, but after a dozen cycles again moved smoothly.

Removing the cartridges from all his magazines he counted a total of 42. He filled one magazine with 30, which he placed on the weapon; the rest he loaded into another magazine that he slipped into his waist pouch. He'd be surprised if the Sten would continue to fire reliably on automatic, as the heat would quickly burn out the remaining lubricant, but he wouldn't know until he tried.

He took a long drink of water then shot a compass bearing to a hill about 5 kilometres north-west. The country was now steeper than he'd expected and he was tiring badly. There was no way he could keep the schedule he'd set for himself. The best he could hope for was to reach the hill before nightfall, then with luck he'd probably be able to make friendly territory sometime in the morning.

A gentle breeze was blowing in off the sea and the cloud cover was thinning. The sun broke through, painting the valley and surrounding hills in the gold-green light that came only after rain. Dennis cinched his belt another notch, took a drink from his canteen, then moving quietly went back to the track. Standing in cover he observed the track for five minutes, his hearing adjusting to the sounds around him. Except for a few birds and the rustle of the wind there was silence. The surface of the track looked unmarked, no footprints or bent grass to indicate it had been used recently.

Stepping out of cover he moved off, the stiffness gradually easing as his muscles warmed. After ten minutes he was walking at a brisk pace, the track winding through the middle of the valley with high grass either side. For an hour he kept going until the valley broadened into an area cut by a wide river, now almost dry. He knew this had to be the Hawain River, which meant he was getting very close to the Australian lines.

Downstream about half a kilometre, a long row of huts were tucked under the trees along the bank. He could see Japanese moving about, and stacks of cut logs and other equipment including motors and piping used to pump water from the river. It looked like a major base camp, so he marked it on his map, taking compass bearings to nearby hills to confirm the position. After waiting to make sure no one was close, he dashed across the stony river bed into the grass on the other side. Pausing to listen and to ensure no one had seen him, he then continued along the track as it climbed back up into dense, hilly country.

After a short climb, the track swung south along a ridge that headed towards the mountains further inland. Checking his map and compass, Dennis found the direction to the hill that was his objective for the day. To stay on course meant leaving the track and climbing down into a valley where he could follow a creek that led up to the hill. It was a short but steep climb through heavy undergrowth, but one he could manage. The sun was now low and he wanted to reach the hill by last light, so after slinging his Sten, he went over the edge, using vines to steady him. After 20 metres the slope became steeper and he scrabbled at the damp earth to stop himself from sliding away. Clutching a thick vine, he was easing down the embankment when, without warning, the vine snapped.

He fell back, tumbling down the slope, crashing through foliage, grasping at vines in a desperate attempt to stop his fall. His right leg tangled in a vine and he jerked to a stop. Heart pounding, he lay on his back, head protruding over a drop of 10 metres. His Sten was dangling by its strap from his right arm, his pack pushed to one side beneath him. Twisting his body he looked around, then froze.

He was on the edge of a large Japanese camp, with maybe a dozen or more huts scattered around among the trees. Directly below him was a long, thatched hut, and outside it a line of Japanese soldiers holding mess kits. They were talking and laughing as they filed into the hut.

As if taunting him, the aroma of cooking food drifted up. For Dennis it was a precarious situation, but the humour of it didn't escape him. If the vine holding his leg snapped, he'd fall through the flimsy roof of the hut into a swarm of Japanese soldiers. For a moment he wondered how they'd react to the sudden arrival of an uninvited dinner guest. His next thought was that if he had to fall, then maybe he could make his entry a little more interesting by coming through the roof, gun blazing.

Slowly he retrieved his weapon, pulling it up on its sling. He managed to wrap it around his shoulder and secure it close to his chest. Glancing back, he watched the last man go into the mess hut—fortunately they'd all been too busy keeping their eyes on the food to look up.

By twisting and wriggling, he was able to move his body back onto the slope. At least now he was concealed by bushes, but every movement dislodged small rocks and clumps of earth that dropped onto the hut's roof. Fortunately the roof was woven from layers of heavy palm fronds, which muffled the sound. But Dennis decided not to risk any further movement—dislodging a large rock would not only alert the soldiers, but also risk hitting him on the way down.

So he remained there, held by one leg, on his back, upside down on the slope, listening to the sounds of happy Japanese eating their evening meal.

It was an hour or more after sunset before the last man left the mess hut. The moon was low in the sky, shedding a soft light that was easy to see by. Dennis watched as the cooks cleared away the table scraps, then emptied them into a pigsty near another hut. When they left, he was able to wriggle around, free his leg, then crawl along the slope until he was at the edge of the encampment.

He couldn't see any sentries, but knew they'd have them somewhere. So slowly he crawled away, circling the area until he found the creek line. There, still on his stomach, he slid down the bank, took a long drink and refilled his canteen. Slithering up the bank, he crawled into the scrub, staying low for 20 metres before standing.

After waiting and listening, hearing nothing but the night sounds of insects, he decided to take advantage of the moonlight and keep moving. Following the creek, walking through low undergrowth about 10 metres from it, he made good time up a narrow valley for another two hours.

As the moon sank behind the mountains, he decided he could go no further. Exhausted, he found a lay-up among bushes away from the creek, removed his gear and made himself comfortable for the night. Before dozing off, he offered thanks to whoever it was who was looking over him. So far his luck had been extraordinary. He hoped it would continue.

Just one more day?

41. SIXTH DIVISION HQ, AITAPE:

20 APRIL, 0700 HOURS

Friday, 20 April 1945 was to be a significant day in various parts of the world. In Berlin, holed up in his bunker, Adolf Hitler celebrated his fifty-sixth birthday as the Russians swarmed towards the city. That same day Nuremberg, where Hitler had staged his massive orchestrated rallies, fell to the Americans who, knowing it was the Führer's birthday, promptly staged their own parade, the giant swastika above Nuremburg Stadium's main arena concealed by a huge stars-and-stripes flag specially made for the occasion. They even flew in a US Army band along with 5000 Hershey bars for distribution to the local population, to remind them that Germany was now under new management.

In the United States, Professor Robert Oppenheimer was reported to have expressed doubts to his colleagues about the dangers of the new atomic weapon they were developing, fearing that when detonated it might trigger a chain reaction in the atmosphere that could see the Earth disappear like a giant seltzer pill.

For Captain Roland McKay, G3 of Sixth Division Intelligence, several events made the day memorable. The first was when he arrived in his office that morning. On his desk was a signal from 1st Army Lae, confirming his promotion to Major. He'd be taking up a new posting on the staff of Sixth Division forward headquarters in the coming Wewak operation.

The promotion gave him some satisfaction. If he'd been a career man, it probably would have been even more satisfying, but he'd already decided that when the war was over he'd be returning to his former profession as a lawyer. Peace-time armies were notoriously neglected and the prospect of sitting around reminiscing about past campaigns and trying to predict future ones held no attraction for him.

The second item arrived half an hour later. The courier C-47 from Darwin had landed early, the result of unexpected tailwinds, and his clerk brought in a file containing the latest analyses from the Allied Intelligence Bureau radio intercept and translation unit in Brisbane. One of these reports had been marked for his attention, so he opened it first.

It was an extract from a situation report transmitted by the Japanese 18th Army in Wewak to their higher HQ in Rabaul. Among the administrative trivia were the names of six Japanese soldiers, all described as being killed in action on Muschu Island. Alongside each name was the date of death: 12, 13, 14, 16 and 17 April. There were no explanations as to how they were killed but he immediately made the connection with Operation Copper. Muschu had been off limits to the Australian Air Force and Navy during this period, so this had to mean that some of the patrol had survived until 17 April, possibly longer. Again there was no mention of more Australian casualties, so there was a chance survivors of the patrol were still on the island.

McKay had talked with Cardew about the results of his venture two nights ago, which was 24 hours after the last killed-in-action date shown in the situtation report. Cardew strongly believed that if any of the patrol were still alive, they would've seen the Boomerang fly past and done their best to make contact with HDML 1321. However, he did admit there was still a remote possibility they were in hiding, unable to signal.

Accordingly, it had been agreed to postpone all action against the island for another seven days. The Navy would keep the rendezvous for a few more nights, and the Air Force would maintain their daily reconnaissance flights. Until further information was received, the patrol was now officially listed as missing in action.

McKay read the situation report again. It wasn't going to make a great deal of difference, but at least they'd accounted for six of the enemy. On the statistics of war, it wasn't a good kill ratio. He dismissed the thought, cursing himself for becoming so mercenary.

Then he noticed that one of the names of the Japanese dead had been flagged by the translation service. It was Colonel Hitoshi Watanabe, killed on 16 April.

So they'd got Watanabe? That was an unexpected bonus. He glanced down the page to the referenced footnote. It was a translation of an administrative message to Rabaul, dated the same day advising that Lieutenant Commander Otomo would replace the deceased Watanabe as the officer commanding the Muschu gun battery.

There it was, the first piece of information positively linking Watanabe to the gun battery and confirming that it was operational. One sentence in a mountain of seemingly innocuous administrative traffic that revealed more information than it should.

Information that, by all indications, had cost eight men's lives.

42. PNG MAINLAND:

20 APRIL, 0800 HOURS

For the first time on the mission Dennis slept well. Being in the high country, the mosquitoes and insects weren't as annoying and this, coupled with deep fatigue, meant he'd slept until dawn. After waking he lay listening to the sounds around him, the birds not nearly as raucous as in the low country. Thankfully there was no indications that the Japanese were anywhere around.

He cleaned his Sten, using the last of the antiseptic cream to lubricate the bolt and spring. Spreading out his map, he tried to fix his position. It looked as if last night's diversion around the Japanese camp had pushed him further inland than expected, but he couldn't be sure until he could get a good view of the surrounding country. Deciding to head west, he moved off, continuing near the creek until it petered out as the terrain steepened. He pushed on up the slope, the rainforest thinning to sparse wooded country covered by low grass.

Low clouds touched the peaks around him and the air grew cold. After two hours he reached the top. Here he had a good view of the surrounding hills, but he couldn't see the coast. Even so, he was able to calculate an approximate position on the map, which put him about 9 kilometres south-east of Dagua. If he was right, it meant he should now be within the Australian forward line of advance, as Dagua was the furthest position south when they'd set out on the mission eight days ago.

So the best plan was to head closer to the coast, which should increase his chances of contacting an Australian patrol.

After taking a compass bearing he moved off, going down the side of the hill back into rainforest, then into a valley before crossing a shallow stream and climbing up the other side. He moved stealthily, alert to the sounds around him, but apart from birds and small animals there was nothing. Once in the distance he heard an aircraft drone past high overhead, but that was the only indication that there were humans anywhere near. It was as if the Japanese had abandoned the area, falling back before the Australian advance.

At about midday he paused at the top of a low hill. To the north he could hear a sound like waves on a beach, mingled with engines—either vehicles or boats, he couldn't be sure. So he decided to make for the sound, figuring there was a good chance it was made by the Australians.

Swinging north along a sloping ridge line, he crossed through grassy country, pausing regularly to listen. Occasionally he heard the sound of engines, but they seemed to be in different places every time he heard them—probably the sound echoing up the valleys, he decided.

After two hours he came to a hill. Climbing to the top, he at last could see the ocean. Almost due north off the coast was Unei Island, and a few kilometres east of it, the long low outline of Paris Island. He now knew exactly where he was—5 kilometres inland from the coast and about 9 kilometres east of Dagua. This was a little further away than he'd expected, but because he'd now fixed his position he could navigate accurately. Choosing a route on the map that curved him north-west, and staying on the ridge lines, he calculated he'd be able to make good time—he'd certainly make the coast in another hour or so.

Setting out, he hadn't gone far when he found a track just off the top of the hill. Running beside it through the trees was a telephone cable. Obviously this was a major route, but after examining the trail he saw it hadn't been used for a very long time, so he decided it was worth the risk.

He removed the Sten's magazine and worked the action to make sure the bolt was free, then replaced the magazine. Walking quickly, he followed the track through open country along the ridge line, then after twenty minutes he stopped. Ahead, coming from where the track wound through a clump of trees, he heard voices. Quietly he moved off the track over the edge of the ridge into long grass and waited.

He didn't recognise the voices: they didn't sound like Japanese, nor did they sound like natives, but he wasn't prepared to risk finding out who they were. Cocking the Sten and applying the safety catch, he went down the side of the ridge, then after 200 metres broke left to confuse anyone who might have followed. He then cut back until he came to flat ground at the bottom of the hill, coming out on the edge of a native garden.

He quickly cut through it to a wide stretch of high kunai grass. He was about to move into the grass when ahead he saw the roof of a very big Papuan hut, possibly 10 metres high and almost 30 metres long. He'd seen these before: they were community huts, usually belonging to a native tribe with several hundred warriors, so if they weren't friendly he could be in big trouble. Suddenly nearby he heard voices.

Crouching down in the high grass he waited. To his left about 10 metres away the kunai grass tops moved. Crouching lower and bringing the Sten up slowly he flicked the change lever to single shot. If he was going to be confronted by hostile Papuans he'd need to make every round count.

A long line of native bearers moved out of the grass into the garden area. They were carrying water cans and passed by only metres away. Then in the middle of the line Dennis saw a soldier. Tall and broad for a Japanese, he looked a big ugly brute. Dressed in jungle greens, his webbing was of the crossed strap pattern and he wore an old felt hat with its side turned up.

Behind him the line of natives kept coming from the kunai grass, some of them jabbering excitedly. The soldier suddenly swung around, a Lee Enfield rifle gripped in his hands, and barked out in a voice Dennis would never forget.

'Keep those natives quiet back there or the bloody Japs will hear them!'

43. SIXTH DIVISION HQ, AITAPE:

20 APRIL, 1600 HOURS

Major McKay looked around the office for the last time. It wasn't much, just some plywood panels dividing the hut, two green filing cabinets, a field desk and a large, somewhat weary map pasted on a wall. It had been home for almost a year now. Strangely, he'd miss it.

In the morning he'd take up his new posting. If all went according to plan, in less than a month he'd have a new office in Wewak. That would be interesting—he wondered who was using it now. Chances were he'd have to rebuild: the size of the supporting fleet and the extent of the pre-landing bombardment would probably level every building in the town.

He'd just buckled up his briefcase and was about to leave when the door opened and a clerk came in with a message flimsy. For a moment he feared it might interrupt his plans for the evening—he was going to have a few farewell drinks at the mess, then pack his kit ready to fly to Dagua in the morning. His successor could handle any of the petty dramas that inevitably arose during the night.

The message was from the 2/7th Commando Company, operating south of Dagua on the advance to Wewak. It had been sent in Slidex, a cumbersome code of the day that meant the message was annoyingly short on detail, posing a hundred questions that left McKay shaking his head in disbelief.

> Survivor Copper patrol, Spr E T Dennis located map reference 0500 2190. In good health.
> For OC, SRD from Spr Dennis: The bastard from the bush has returned.

EPILOGUE

At Sixth Division HQ, Sapper Dennis's unexpected appearance on the mainland was initially greeted with disbelief.

While Operation Copper had been classified as secret, even in the most disciplined of military environments word spreads like ripples in a pond, so the fact that the patrol had been missing was common knowledge among most HQ staff.

Before long there was the inevitable speculation about what had happened and how Dennis had managed to survive—there was even a rather absurd suggestion that he might have been an elaborate Japanese 'plant', but all this was quickly dismissed when further information began arriving.

There was no doubt that it was NX 73110, Sapper E.T. (Mick) Dennis, somewhat worse for wear, but definitely the larrikin himself. One of the reasons his *bona fides* were so quickly established was the fact that when Dennis had come across the Australian patrol, the very first soldier he'd seen turned out to be an old friend—Sergeant 'Fatty' Osborne of the 2/7th Commandos, with whom he'd served in Salamaua and Mubo in 1942 and 1943.

Taken to the 2/7th forward base camp, Dennis was immediately among old friends, most of whom he hadn't seen since they'd pulled out of New Guinea in 1943. After some food, which he immediately threw up, he gave a quick outline of his story to the Lieutenant in Command—by now almost the entire Sixth Division HQ was clamouring over the radio for more information and he was anxious to get them off his back. It was as though they feared Dennis would suddenly roll over and die without explaining his extraordinary feat of survival.

After this initial debrief, Dennis set off with a heavy escort on a two-hour march back to the main base at Dagua. There he was given a small meal, which this time he held down, and he was then questioned by the unit's intelligence officer. The information he'd gained during his mainland trek was of particular interest, as this was the area into which they were now advancing.

From Dagua, late in the afternoon, Dennis was driven by jeep to But. Here at last he was able to relax a little. He was given a long hot shower, clean uniform and a going over by the medical officer. It was estimated he'd lost almost 12 kilograms during his ordeal, but apart from coral gashes and some other cuts and assorted bruising plus two very sore feet, he was in good physical condition. After further debriefings, he was flown the following day by Auster back to Aitape.

For the next two days he was thoroughly debriefed by officers from the Allied Intelligence Bureau, Sixth Division Intelligence and the Aitape SRD detachment commander. Every point of his story was checked in detail, much of his information about Muschu being verified by aerial reconnaissance in the following days. The SRD had already begun an investigation into the operation, in an effort to learn from it for future operations, and Dennis's information was vital.

From his story, it was evident the patrol had been plagued by bad luck from the moment they'd left HDML 1321. The currents that forced them south of their original objective hadn't been accurately assessed, and this was just the beginning of a chain of events over which they had little control. The tide information was correct, but the currents swirled around the island in an unpredictable pattern that was impossible to factor into the mission without extensive local knowledge of the area. Ironically, although the currents swept them onto the reef west of Cape Barabar, it also gave them a temporary reprieve—as they'd discovered, their intended landing zone was right beneath a major defensive position.

As suspected, the ATR4 and SCR36 radios proved unsuitable for this operation due to their susceptibility to water damage. However, Dennis went to great lengths to point out that what might have saved seven men's lives wasn't necessarily better radios. If they'd had waterproof torches they could have signalled the HDML, arranged a pick-up and left the island that first night. Instead, they'd tried to make do with standard-issue torches bound with electrical tape. The torches had leaked, short-circuited and the water destroyed the batteries within a few hours of them landing. These were simple pieces of equipment that the supply system had failed to provide and for that there was no excuse.

After interviewing Dennis, the Aitape SRD Commander believed there was still a remote possibility that some of Lieutenant Barnes's group had survived. Considering the distance the current had taken Dennis, there was a chance it had carried some or all of them north of Cape Wom, so the Navy's patrol boats were requested to patrol close to the shore where possible. They were also tasked to check nearby islands and as far away as Vokeo. However, no trace of them was ever found. They were later assumed to have drowned or been taken by sharks.

As for the other missing personnel—Signallers Hagger, Chandler and Sergeant Max Weber—Dennis knew very little about their fate. The last he'd seen of them was approximately midday on 14 April after they'd all gone back to the equipment cache to retrieve the radios. It was then while returning to their lay-up near the bomb crater that they'd encountered the ambush, and the resulting action was a confused blur. While Dennis held off the Japanese using the Sten, the other three had scattered, and he was certain they'd escaped. He'd checked the rendezvous later in the day and again the following morning, but there was no sign of them having been there. On that point he was absolutely certain.

The SRD was already aware of the fate of two of the group, their deaths being revealed by radio intercept as having occurred on 17 April although their names or the exact circumstances of their deaths weren't mentioned in the report. During the debrief Dennis wasn't informed of this, as to do so would reveal the existence of the radio intercept unit. After the Japanese surrendered, their fate could be determined, but until then the file would remain open.

After the debriefing, Dennis was flown to Madang. Here the medical officer gave him a thorough going over, then told the assorted intelligence agencies and anyone else who thought they would like to have Dennis explain his story again to leave him alone. He needed to rest and anything else they wanted to know could wait. The medical officer recommended him for immediate home leave.

For the next six days Dennis rested, doing little but sleeping and eating. While he was at Madang, the Officer Commanding 1st Australian Army, South-West Pacific, General Vernon Sturdee, after being briefed on his ordeal, recommended Dennis for the Military Medal. A small ceremony took place on the parade ground and the citation read out, but Dennis would have to wait until after the war before he could receive his award. There were several hurdles yet to be crossed before the way was cleared—one of them apparently caused by an old antagonist who'd recently been shuffled out of Sixth Division HQ to an administrative post in Brisbane, where he attempted to delay the award process.

On day seven, Dennis was pleasantly surprised when HDML 1321 cruised into the harbour. The celebration that followed he later modestly described as being 'memorably rowdy'.

The next day Dennis boarded HDML 1321 and they motored down the coast to Lae, where he reported to the SRD that afternoon. More debriefing sessions followed, and again Dennis stressed that for the want of waterproof torches seven lives might have been saved.

The following day he was flown by C-47 to Brisbane, then on to Sydney.

For Mick Dennis, the war was finally over.

■ ■ ■

The information Dennis provided was put to good use within hours of his rescue. Even though he'd been almost constantly pursued, he'd never forgotten the aim of his mission. He'd continually maintained his notebook and maps, marking enemy positions, sightings, structures—anything he considered might be valuable later.

The first conclusion arrived at by Sixth Division after examining all the data was that invading Muschu wouldn't be worth the casualties that would inevitably result. The defences were too well prepared, and the maze of tracks on the island indicated that the enemy enjoyed a significant home-ground advantage. It would be much simpler just to isolate the island and keep the enemy neutralised there.

Meanwhile, to avoid having an enemy literally within shooting distance of Wewak during and after the Australian landings, Sixth Division drew up plans to eliminate as many of the enemy defences as possible.

The aerial bombing of Muschu was extensive. A number of large raids using 30 or more B-24 Liberators hit the southern coast line, one of these concentrating on the location of the naval guns. Tactical Reconnaissance sorties later confirmed that the bombs were on target and the area was extensively cratered. Muschu was also heavily shelled by Australian Navy sloops and corvettes. HDMLs, including HDML 1321, then prowled the coastal waters targeting areas located by Dennis with their machine guns and cannons. Beauforts from Tadji continued to strike targets on the island up to and after the invasion. Interrogation of Japanese prisoners after the war indicated that this period was particularly hazardous for the garrison, which until then had enjoyed a relatively peaceful existence.

On 10 May 1945, the landings at Wewak went ahead. Australian losses were 451 killed and 1163 wounded. By comparison, 7200 Japanese died in the campaign.

During the landings, the guns of Muschu remained silent.

■ ■ ■

The war dragged on, with the Japanese withdrawing further into the remote high country, hemmed in and harassed by the Australians advancing from Aitape, Wewak and Lae. On 15 August, after atomic bombs were dropped on Hiroshima and Nagasaki, Japan surrendered.

After the close of hostilities, there were loose ends to tidy up, mountains of paperwork to be completed and investigations to be conducted. The SRD had a few loose ends of its own, including the fate of the seven missing men from Operation Copper. The circumstances behind their deaths were to be confirmed, and their bodies located and buried with due ceremony.

Major Cardew was given the task of carrying out the investigation. In September 1945, he travelled to Muschu Island to interview the Japanese officer who commanded the island during the period of the operation. Muschu by then had been turned into an internment camp housing almost 13,000 Japanese soldiers awaiting processing before being repatriated to Japan.

After a month's work, during which he interviewed the commander of the island and other officers and soldiers present during Operation Copper, Cardew concluded that the four Australian commandos who'd set out to swim to the mainland had been lost as previously assumed. The fate of the three others was clouded by a report from local islanders, who'd fled to the mainland claiming that they'd witnessed the execution of the Australians, then seen their bodies mutilated by the Japanese.

Cardew continued his investigation and finally decided that these claims were groundless. The grave where the three men were buried was located, their bodies exhumed, then moved to Wewak for medical examination, to be later interred in the Lae War Cemetery.

The final report was compiled by Major Cardew in October, then confirmed by Headquarters 1st Australian Army in November 1945. The file was then closed.

■ ■ ■

Over 40 years later, when shown a copy of this investigation, Mick Dennis disagreed with the findings concerning the deaths of Chandler, Hagger and Weber. Out of respect for their relatives he'd remained silent on the subject, believing it would serve no real purpose to reopen the case. He firmly believed the Japanese executed the three men, then mutilated their bodies. Someone—probably one of the Japanese commanders or his officers—then contrived a cover story.

According to Major Cardew, the Japanese commander of the island stated that two of the Australians were tracked after escaping the ambush, and were then shot dead while trying to operate their radios. From the description of the two men it was assumed they were probably Signallers Chandler and Hagger. The location wasn't specified, but reported to be 'somewhere in the area of the water hole'.

A third Australian was found dead later the same day, near the poisoned water-filled bomb crater that had been their rendezvous.

The Japanese stated that all the bodies were left where they had fallen for over a month. They also claimed that they had not searched the bodies or removed any documents or identity tags. This in itself is peculiar behaviour: it is normal procedure to search enemy dead for identification and intelligence purposes.

The two men shot while using the radio would possibly have been carrying the mission codebooks and signals instructions—potentially valuable information for Japanese intelligence. Even if they'd ditched them earlier, any Japanese soldier worth his pay would realise that Australian soldiers with radios were valuable captives. Armed with only .38 Smith & Wesson pistols they probably would have been easily taken prisoner, especially if they were outnumbered or surprised. At the very least their bodies would have been searched. Similarly, any competent commander would have reported back to his immediate HQ, giving details of the action and information about any enemy killed. Captain Tomei's rather lame explanation that he had no idea why the bodies were left where they fell for over a month simply doesn't ring true.

And assuming the Japanese commander's explanation that the third man (Sergeant Weber) was wounded and then crawled to the rendezvous where he died was true, why didn't Dennis find the body when he returned later that day to search for his mates? Dennis had also checked around the rendezvous, including the concealed area they'd already used as a lay-up—a place they'd agreed was suitable to set up the radios. He didn't find any bodies then, nor the following morning when he returned to check the area before setting out to escape the island.

There are also other inconsistencies with Captain Tomei and Captain Temura's statements, but unfortunately after more than 60 years, nothing can be proved, and most of those involved are now gone.

However, there are still islanders who remember the commando raid. Villager Michael Sumari recalls:

> Australians landed at Som Point, right over there. They had a Bren Gun and .303 rifles and went around the island shooting Japanese

> on the island. The Japanese were eating lunch and they caught them by surprise. Word spread that they were there and they tracked them down. When the Australians saw us islanders, they would say 'We have come here to save you,' but we did not know what to do. The Japanese found them and killed three and one [E.T. Dennis] swam back to Cape Wom and he was safe.

This statement suggests a possible clue to the fate of Chandler, Hagger and Weber. Even though there are inaccuracies concerning the weapons carried by the Australians and the patrol's landing area, which can probably be attributed to confusion over the years, what is significant is Sumari's description of the patrol's reaction when they sighted the islanders: 'We have come here to save you'.

The natives on Muschu were sympathetic towards the Japanese and it's likely they were being used as trackers. If Michael Sumari's statement is based on fact, then it's possible that Signallers Chandler and Hagger were discovered by a native. Perhaps they tried to persuade the tracker to keep their location secret, but he had second thoughts or told his friends and the information was passed on to the Japanese. What hasn't been explained is why the Japanese reported that casualties were still being inflicted on them up until the afternoon of 17 April, one of these being Lieutenant Colonel Watanabe. Radio intercept indicates Watanabe was being escorted by a Japanese squad when they were ambushed at the eastern end of the island—probably by one Australian commando during the afternoon of 16 April. At this time Mick Dennis was at the western end of Muschu, resting up before his night crossing of the strait to the mainland.

Was the squad ambushed by Sergeant Max Weber? At first this seems unlikely, as Weber would only have been armed with a .38 Smith & Wesson, hardly a weapon one would use to take on ten or more Japanese soldiers. However, it's also possible he had the remaining Welrod. Could he have seen an opportunity to inflict more Japanese casualties? Hidden near the track he may have realised Watanabe was of importance and used the silenced weapon with great effect. The result would be the confusion reported by the Australian radio intercept unit.

One final mystery concerning the fate of the three men relates to Signaller Michael Hagger. Although Major Cardew concluded that he was shot along with Signaller Chandler while they were attempting to get the radios working, and that his remains were returned to the Lae War Cemetery for burial, Michael Hagger remained listed as Missing in Action for some time after the war. For more than a year afterwards, the Military Police continued to arrive unannounced at his parents' home in Victoria to search for him.

Why would the Military Police conduct a search for a soldier who was known to be buried in a war cemetery? Was this an example of the military bureaucracy gone cruelly wrong, or did they have additional information? One can hardly believe Chandler somehow escaped the island and made his way back to Australia, yet the family was subjected to this indignity many times without explanation or apology.

The truth about the fate of these men may never be known.

History reveals, that the guns of Muschu, which had been at the centre of the ill-fated operation, were untouched by the subsequent Australian bombing. For many years after the war they stood with their barrels elevated and ammunition in ready-lockers around them. Eventually they were picked over by locals and souvenir hunters, anything removable whisked away to private collections or scrap merchants.

The guns themselves remain intact to this day, partly concealed by jungle and looking as if they are still waiting to be fired.

APPENDIX

The following report is the result of the investigation conducted by Major R.A. Cardew, Services Reconnaissance Department, into the loss of seven men during Z Special, Operation Copper, 11-20 April 1945. The report has been copied verbatim, with corrections to spelling only. The original document source is in the Australian War Memorial Archives.

In this report, Major Cardew refers to Cape Sabar (see p. 241). It is believed that this is either an accidental misinterpretation of the name Cape Barabar as marked on the operational map or a localised abbreviation. The actual landing site was on the beach about a kilometre south-west of Cape Barabar. The maps used for the mission were compiled by the US Army Corps of Engineers from aerial photographs, but there were also German maps created before World War I, and subsequent Australian adaptations. The proliferation of maps was the source of some confusion at the time and resulted in different names being used for many prominent features on Muschu Island and the New Guinea coast.

REPORT ON INVESTIGATIONS OF MISSING PERSONNEL—MUSCHU ISLAND

10 OCT 1945

To: C.S.

From: Major R.A.C. Cardew

Subject: REPORT ON INVESTIGATIONS OF MISSING PERSONNEL—**MUSCHU PARTY**

The following personnel were members of an S.R.D. party from Group 'C' who were inserted into MUSCHU Island, T.N.G. [Territory of New Guinea], on the night 11/12 Apr 1945:

Lt	BARNES J.J.
Lt	GUBBAY A.R.
Sgt	WEBER M.F.M.
L/Cpl	WALKLATE S.H.
Pte	EAGLETON R.E.
Spr	DENNIS E.T.

Sig. HAGGER M.

Sig. CHANDLER J.R.

I was instructed by C.O. 'Z' Special Unit to proceed to H.Q. 6 Aust. Div. to make investigations in an effort to trace the seven missing personnel of this party (Spr DENNIS was the only member of the party to return safely to our lines). I arrived at WEWAK, the location of 6 Aust. Div. on 13 Sept 45. There I contacted the G.O.C. G1 of 6 Aust Div., O.C. ANGAU Det., WEWAK, and O.C. A.I.B. Det., WEWAK. All the above officers advised me that investigations and interrogations of the enemy had been carried out in an attempt to locate the whereabouts of the missing personnel, but that no trace could be found.

About five days prior to my arrival all the natives of MUSCHU Island had been withdrawn to the mainland in the vicinity of the HAWAIN River. This was done as it was intended that the whole of MUSCHU Island would be used as a P.W. Camp for the enemy.

On 14 Sep 45, I obtained permission from all concerned to proceed to HAWAIN River to personally interrogate the abovementioned natives. These natives had been very pro-Japanese and, as a result, were not inclined to make any information available on any matter in the fear that they would be implicated as War Criminals with the Japanese in any atrocities committed in the area. However, by using subterfuge methods I was able to obtain the following information:

(i) That a party of unknown numbers had landed on the eastern tip of MUSCHU Island (Cape SABAR) about the middle of April, 1945.

(ii) Three of the party were ambushed and killed by Japanese naval members of the Island garrison, approximately three days later.

(iii) The name of the native who accompanied the enemy patrol which ambushed these personnel.

(iv) The name of the native who was fired at by Spr DENNIS (according to his report).

(v) The approximate location of the site of the ambush.

(vi) The approximate position of the foldboat hideout.

(vii) The whereabouts of 1 ATR4A wireless set and 1 Welrod.

(viii) That the bodies of the three personnel were mutilated by having their legs, arms and heads cut off by enemy troops after the personnel had been shot (this latter information proved incorrect).

(ix) The natives had no knowledge of the whereabouts of the remaining four missing personnel nor had they seen them or heard of them at any stage of the action.

(x) The area in which the operation took place was under enemy Naval control.

On 15 Sep 45, accompanied by the native who was with the enemy patrol during the action, a MANUS native who had heard of the operation, and an interpreter in Japanese, I proceeded to Cape SABAR on MUSCHU Island and there located:

(i) The foldboat hideout.

(ii) The position at which two of the party were ambushed and killed while endeavouring to work their W/T set.

(iii) The water-hole mentioned in Spr DENNIS' report where the remains of the third body were found.

In reference to (i) above, odd pieces of dowelling were found in the area of the foldboat hideout.

In reference to (ii) above, pieces of human skeletons and clothing were found in the area of the ambush.

In reference to (iii) above, again pieces of human skeleton were found.

All remains were collected to take back to the 7 Aust. War Graves Unit at WEWAK.

Later that day in making a reconnaissance of the Island, I ran into a Japanese Naval patrol and questioned them on their knowledge of the shooting of the three personnel. They told me that a Capt. TOMEI, the Japanese Naval officer who was in command of that area, had full knowledge of the matter and would answer any questions necessary. I proceeded to the Western tip of the Island to MARCHESA Bay where Capt. TOMEI was located and interrogated him. He said that he was not in a position to answer my questions, but that the naval Commander of the Island, a Capt. TEMURA, would be in a position to give the full information required. I then proceeded to Capt. TEMURA's H.Q., which were three miles distant, and interrogated him. He advised that he had only taken over command of the Island on the day of the landing of our party and therefore was not fully in the picture in the matter but that Capt. TOMEI would answer all questions. I immediately put Capt. TEMURA under arrest and returned to MARCHESA Bay to put Capt. TOMEI under arrest but found that he had, in the meantime, returned to the Eastern tip of the Island.

Owing to sea transport difficulties I was not able to contact Capt. TOMEI until the following day, whereupon I interrogated both Capt. TOMEI and Capt. TEMURA together, the outcome being that Capt. TEMURA instructed Capt. TOMEI to give all the information required and to facilitate in the recovering of the bodies. From this interrogation the following information was received:

(i) The party had landed on the night 11/12 Apr 45 at Cape SABAR.

(ii) The enemy had suffered as casualties from action by our party, six killed and two wounded and one, possibly two, MGs destroyed (owing to the length of time between the landing of the party and the time of interrogations, Capt. TOMEI could not remember the exact details of the MGs).

(iii) A Japanese patrol found one dead Japanese soldier on the beach at Cape WARBU. This patrol then proceeded immediately eastwards along the beach and located the foldboats, by which time they realized an enemy party had landed and the alarm was given. An ambush was arranged over the foldboats; patrols were dispatched to various parts of the Island, and a general search was made.

(iv) Approximately two days later two of our personnel were surprised by an enemy party while trying to make communication with their W/T Set. The two personnel were shot dead at a range of approximately 30 yards. One of them had in his possession a Welrod.

(v) The following day another of our personnel was found

dead at the water-hole mentioned by Spr DENNIS' report, having apparently died of wounds which had occurred in a clash with the party the day before. The bodies were not searched and were left lying where they fell for one month. The remains were then collected and buried in a common grave North of Cape SABAR. Capt. TOMEI could give no reason as to why the bodies were not buried immediately.

(vi) While the bodies were left on the ground part of one of them was blown to pieces during a bombing raid.

(vii) The wireless set and Welrod were brought to Capt. TOMEI's H.Q. and then they passed them on to Capt. TEMURA's H.Q.

(viii) Capt. TOMEI stated that the personnel were not searched or mutilated in any way after death.

On completion of the interrogation Capt. TOMEI led me to the common grave of the three personnel. There I observed the nearly complete skeletons of three personnel, one of the skulls having a bullet wound above the left ear. Also from this grave was dug up one serviceable oil bath prismatic compass and odd pieces of equipment and clothing. The grave was clean, well laid out and marked with three headstones. The bones, on my examination, did not appear to have been fractured in any way as had been stated by the natives.

Neither Capt. TEMURA nor Capt. TOMEI had any knowledge at all of Lt BARNES, Lt GUBBAY, L/Cpl WALKLATE, Pte EAGLETON or Spr DENNIS. However, they estimated that, owing to the extent of operations of the party, approximately 16-20 personnel had been landed. They did not know that

Spr DENNIS had escaped and were quite surprised to know that there were still four personnel missing.

The bodies were taken to the WEWAK War Cemeteries (7 Aust. War Graves) where I arranged for a burial service and photographer to take photos of the graves. Unfortunately, I was unable to identify individually the three bodies but from the following information and deductions I presume them to be Sgt WEBER, Sig. CHANDLER and Sig. HAGGER:

(i) Spr DENNIS stated that four personnel had set out on individual logs to contact HDML 1321, i.e. Lt BARNES, Lt GUBBAY, L/Cpl WALKLATE, Pte EAGLETON.

(ii) The three personnel remaining with him were Sgt WEBER, Sig. CHANDLER and Sig. HAGGER.

(iii) Spr DENNIS stated in his opinion that these three personnel had been killed by the enemy in the action and position described in his report which was, as far as possible, confirmed by Capt. TEMURA and Capt. TOMEI.

(iv) It is most probable that the two personnel working the W/T set were the two signallers.

(v) The four personnel who set out on logs would not have landed at their point of embarkation owing to the strong currents prevailing in that area.

Aust. War Graves are making a full investigation into the matter of identification of the bodies and they hope to obtain satisfactory results.

Owing to the lack of sea transport for the next two days I was held up at WEWAK. On the following day I proceeded to WALLIS Island, West of MUSCHU Island, where I interrogated the native chiefs and other members of the Island, but they had no knowledge whatever of the operation nor of any of the personnel concerned. This is quite understandable as these natives were not friendly disposed towards the MUSCHU natives nor the enemy and would make as little contact with MUSCHU as possible.

The following three days I spent in making a search and contact of natives on KAIRIRU Island just North of MUSCHU. These natives had knowledge of the three personnel all being killed on MUSCHU but were completely unaware of the existence of any further personnel. Throughout all the interrogations of the natives I am convinced, from my own personal knowledge of their nature, that they spoke the truth in all but a few minor details, in fact, eventually, they had a tendency to exaggerate in certain matters in their endeavour to help. I am also convinced that no atrocities were committed against our party by the enemy and that the information that they eventually gave me was true, to the best of their knowledge. In fact, once they realized that they would not be marked as war criminals, they were eager to give all the information in their power.

As regards the four missing personnel, the only conclusion I can come to is that they lost their lives by drowning at sea. It is to be remembered that they set out separately on logs approximately 2000 hours at night in waters with very strong currents—up to 2 to 3 knots—and that by daylight they were probably washed well off the coast and either succumbed through exhaustion or were drowned or taken by sharks.

Prior to my closing up of Group 'C' in Jun 45, I had personally searched VOKEO and VALIF Islands, lying to the

North-East of MUSCHU, and there were no signs of them having landed there. Therefore I did not consider it necessary to make a further search of these Islands.

(Signed) Major R.A.C. CARDEW

AUTHOR'S NOTE

The story of Operation Copper and the ordeal of Sapper Mick Dennis has taken me over 40 years to write. Mick Dennis is my uncle and when I was a youth I'd often heard my family talking about his and other relatives' experiences during the war. Mick's story, though, was always discussed with a certain amount of awe, with voices hushed whenever I came into hearing range.

I'd asked my uncle a number of times to tell me about his experiences and being a modest person, his explanations always tended to be very brief. The early impression I gained from these discussions was of a visit to a tropical island for a quick look around to see what the enemy was up to, then a rather long swim home.

It wasn't until 1990, when Mick loaned me his diaries, that I learned the truth about Operation Copper. I think he figured by then I'd matured sufficiently to be able to approach the subject objectively. I'd spent 10 years in the Army, served in Vietnam, been married, had children, done all those things that in theory contribute to grey hairs and wisdom. I found his story fascinating and I suppose having had my own experiences of jungle warfare and having lost several of my own mates in Vietnam I could better understand what he'd endured.

By then, there'd been a number of unit histories written that mentioned Operation Copper, along with many of the other Z Special Operations conducted during the war—the most notable of course being Operation Jaywick. Unfortunately these tended to briefly summarise the events, or merely list the ordeal in chronological order, much in the way of the official histories. While competently written, I felt that none of them really did Operation Copper justice.

I'd just published a book about the Vietnam War and after showing my editor sample chapters the editor agreed it would make an exciting story. In 1992, I visited the Australian War Museum's (AWM's) research centre and they offered me every assistance. Over the following years I continued my research, visiting the AWM many times and collecting more data. One difficulty I'd had with the story was trying to obtain background information into the reasons behind the mission, the personnel involved and a range of small yet vital facts that filled in many of the blanks in the narrative. Even with the AWM's excellent facility, driving to Canberra for research involved time that business commitments wouldn't allow.

The project stalled until 2000. Although I regretted the delay, in many ways it was a godsend. Suddenly I had a new research tool at my disposal—the internet. The AWM went online and their database grew; eventually, all the headquarters war diaries covering the period of Operation Copper became available. The internet also allowed me to obtain accounts from veterans and their unit associations in Australia and Japan—even information on the radios and weapons used by Z Special were now online.

This information allowed me to approach the story in a totally different manner. All military ventures have reasons behind them. What were the reasons behind Operation Copper? Who were the personalities involved?

What were the Japanese doing when the Australians infiltrated the island? Who were they?

The internet, while providing many of the answers, also opened up more questions. Although it gave me background and additional information on Operation Copper, there were still many gaps that were impossible to fill. Fortunately most of these were minor details, so where possible I've made my own assessment as to what occurred and filled them in accordingly. I don't claim to be 100 per cent accurate as the information has either been lost or has been buried by time; however, the recounting of Mick Dennis's journey comes mostly from his own diaries and from discussions over the past 30 or more years with him and members of our family.

Many people believe war diaries kept by military units are 100 per cent accurate and treat them as if they are the ultimate reference source. My experience in Vietnam and speaking with Second World War veterans who'd maintained such diaries disputes this. Many commanders were simply too busy fighting the war to worry about filling in the paperwork each evening. Certainly they made an effort to do so, but the diaries at all levels took second place to the business of war.

This also applies to HQ diaries. In my research I found inaccuracies with many entries, usually only a minor detail, but often enough to open a different thread of investigation. One instance were the entries listing the activities of the naval patrol vessels during Operation Copper. Sometimes they were referred to as an HDML, at other times a Fairmile, and when crosschecked with crew logs it became apparent that someone was confusing their vessel types and numbers. Army personnel are generally ignorant about ship types—vessels come in various sizes and are usually painted grey, with a blunt and a sharp end and hopefully structures in between that include weapons and a beer fridge.

Often the diaries were compiled by clerks using hastily written notes handed to them by various commanders, and some of the details of these entries became guesswork. While many former staff officers will deny this, the Australian 1st Army HQ war diaries themselves contain several entries during 1944-45 appealing for sub-units to pay more attention to accuracy when compiling the diaries!

Although such errors made little difference to the outcome of the war, for the individuals concerned it can be annoying to be credited with deeds they haven't done or see credit mistakenly given to someone else.

I've attempted to straighten out confusing details, but sometimes the picture is just too clouded by the passage of time and unreliable memories. Expecting veterans of a war that is now more than 60 years over to be completely accurate is being unrealistic. So I apologise in advance for any errors or incorrect assumptions I may have made.

Another point I need to make is that when researching Operation Copper, I not only found many differences in the way the Army operates then and now, but also many similarities. Z Special had its supporters and its critics. Some of its operations were failures, many more were successful.

Although Mick Dennis probably believes otherwise, Operation Copper was a success. Many of the techniques used by Australian Special Forces today evolved from lessons learned the hard way by soldiers like Mick Dennis and the men of Operation Copper.

ACKNOWLEDGMENTS

To acknowledge everyone who assisted me with this book over such a long gestation period would be impossible. First in line though would have to be Mick Dennis, family legend and gentleman. Although I've never told him, the knowledge that he'd 'done it' was always in my mind during my tour of Vietnam. He'd set the benchmark and although I wanted to go home only 24 hours after arriving at Nui Dat, I knew if I turned to jelly I'd be letting him and my family down.

Next would be my late uncle, George (Gus) Golding. George was an irrepressible character with whom Mick had a friendship that lasted more than 60 years. I was only privy to *some* of the escapades George and Mick got up to over that time—mostly from George after a bottle or two. George taught me to box and shoot and, once during the mid-1970s he told me about Mick's experience—and also the rather eerie story of a night in 1945 when his two sisters suddenly awoke believing Mick was in great danger. It was George who originally sparked my desire to eventually tell Mick's story. So thanks George—wherever you are.

Of great assistance has been the Australian War Memorial's online archives. Before that the staff of their research centre were always helpful and courteous. I encourage the Government to continue funding their projects as it's vital we preserve and learn from the lessons of the past. The availability of the internet gives everyone a chance to delve into the archives and Australia is probably unique in being able to eventually have all our military records online.

Major Ronald Smith (retired) deserves special acknowledgment. His was the first face I saw when I marched into my first army unit, 16th Army Light Aircraft Squadron, back in April 1966. That was scary. We've been friends ever since and got up to our own brand of mischief, including landing Army aeroplanes in places where aeroplanes were never meant to go. I didn't know it then but Ron had flown Beauforts and Beaufighters in the New Guinea campaign and managed to safely ditch his crippled aircraft after getting it shot full of holes around Wewak during a raid on the town. He'd also flown over Muschu Island many times and his descriptions of the island and the surrounding coastal areas provided valuable background to the narrative.

Captain Owen Eather, long-time friend who I met in Vietnam and once accidentally saluted because he looked so pukka I mistook him for the Task Force Commander, has provided valuable support. His knowledge of the New Guinea campaign is I believe second to none.

Hitoshi Nakatsu, whose relatives also fought in the New Guinea campaign, has been especially helpful in providing me with information about the Japanese forces and their intelligence services at the time. He's also given insight into the possible characters and motivation of some of the commanders in the area. He's handled my questions with dignity and patience and put me in contact with other Japanese families who had relatives in New Guinea. Sometimes we forget that our opponents had families too.

John Arthur, formerly of the Royal Navy, was also instrumental in convincing me the book should be written. His stories of sending young seamen to 'fetch buckets of steam from the fog locker' were a reminder of how naive young soldiers (and sailors) can be. I fell for the same stunt myself when as a brand-new second lieutenant, on day one in my new unit, Major Ron Smith ordered me to go and get issued with a new blue beret from the squadron's 'Far Q'. I spent two hours wandering around the base making an idiot of myself asking directions to this mysterious, non-existent Quartermaster's store.

Geoff Black, a former Fairmile crewman whose craft participated in the search for the missing patrol, was very informative in describing the activities of the Fairmiles and the HDMLs during that period. His-self published work *Against all Odds* is worthy of reading and in addition goes into much of the background of the 2/5th Commando Company and its campaign around Mubo and Wau in 1943. The 2/5th was Mick Dennis's original unit before he joined Z Special, and their stand against the Japanese has tended to be overshadowed by the Kokoda campaign.

Justin Taylan, webmaster of www.pacificwrecks.com, has been particularly helpful in providing photos of Muschu and information about the natives who were on the island during Operation Copper. Contact with Justin has added some interesting twists to the narrative.

Peter Dunn, of www.diggerhistory.info, has provided valuable information. The Digger History site has over 4000 online pages and gave me important details on the somewhat tangled structure of the Allied Intelligence Bureau, the Special Operations Executive and the Services Reconnaissance Department.

There are many more—you know who you are and I thank you for your persistence. For some it's been a very long wait.

THE GUNS OF MUSCHU WEBSITE

Learn more about Operation Copper by visiting
www.gunsofmuschu.com

This website contains photos and descriptions of equipment, weapons and tactics used by Australia's Z Special forces, with links to the Australian War Memorial's archives where the official war diaries and the original maps used for the operation can be viewed.